# *Koranic Verses*

# *Koranic Verses,*

A Frank Study of The Koran.
How the Koran Is Honored & Dishonored In Practice.
Understanding Islam's History.

## By Walter Lamp, JD (Yale)

RunningLight Publishing Company,
Reno, Nevada

Lamp, Walter
*Koranic Verses, A Frank Study of The Koran/* Walter Lamp

First Edition

Includes bibliographical references and index.

1 Koran – Scripture.      2 Islam – Theology – Doctrines.
3 History – Islam.        4 Religion – Hierarchy – Clergy.
5 Muhammed.  6 Hadiths.  7 Shariah.  8 Fundamentalism.
9 Extremism.   10 Terrorism.   11 Tolerance.   12 Law.
13 Political Science - Separation Religion/State.   14 Israel.

ISBN-13:  978-0-9816681-2-3 (pbk.)

Library of Congress Control Number: 2008943533

BP 130,  297.122 LAM 2009          10 9 8 7 6 5 4 3 2-1

Printed in the United States of America

# Table of Contents

# Introduction

A religion is essentially no more and no less than its Scripture, with all else being irrelevant. The moment a Scripture is accepted as being divine and eternal, no man-made commentary or historical context can be reliable enough or have the status to either stand against or elucidate that divine source. Scripture is the very core of a religion and only its words define the religion.

It is within this sense that I explore the Koran as a doctor of jurisprudence would explore a law to determine what it actually says. There cannot be anything like legislative intent behind a Scripture, for nobody can know the mind of God except through what He[1] has said in His Scripture. Having been written or inspired by God Himself, the words in a Scripture should be and are plain enough to get His message through. We can't do better.

---

[1] Ancient writings, like the Koran, generally use the male gender. To avoid complexity of presentation, the author uses words like "his" or "man" to encompass both genders unless the context demands otherwise.

I accept the plain words of the Koran as being perfectly adequate to explain the Islamic religion without the need for man-made interpretations. Besides, such interpretations could not stand against the divine words of God if the interpretations are in conflict with His Koran, or, alternatively, they would be superfluous if in agreement with the Koran. Either way, the interpretations would be irrelevant and of no account.

This book was written with two perspectives in mind; the Western perspective and the Muslim perspective.

From the Western perspective; I am most pleased to show the Koran as being kind and tolerant, and not the cause of all the war and mayhem conducted in the name of Islam. There is no prescription in the Koran for perpetual war, as I had initially feared when I started my studies, but, to the contrary, the Koran itself does stand for peace. I am able to prove it and also show that Westerners erroneously criticize the Koran and Islam for many other things that are not true. This book explains the Koran to Westerners, reliably, adequately, and with surprising simplicity.

From the Muslim perspective, being a non-Muslim myself, I do not presume to speak to the learned. Rather, I address those Muslims who have not studied the Koran or just studied it by rote and are in danger of being misled by firebrand clerics having extremist agendas.

I bring my modernly worded quotations of the gist (essence and substance) of Koranic verses to the forefront of the issues discussed so that everyone can see and understand what the Koran actually says, and I invite the Arabic speaking to check it out against the Koran. By so emphasizing what the Koran actually says, I am able to highlight the only too obvious disconnects between what the Koran says and what the disobedient do or say to do. I then explore what is happening to ordinary Muslims, how they are being exploited by their fellows and how they are losing the key franchise the Koran gave them.

The first chapter, *"What The Koran Actually Says,"* tells it as it is, correcting misconceptions found amongst both Westerners and Muslims. A non-Muslim can do this because the Koran proves to be very clear and, as the Koran itself says, it does explain all things. It is most easy for someone without baggage or preconceived notions to see the disconnect between the practice and the words in the Koran.

The disconnect shows that some Muslims are obviously disobeying the Koran, probably not intentionally because they are likely doing what they are being told by other Muslims. From the Western perspective, only by understanding what the Koran actually says, without bias or slant, can Westerners begin to understand Islam.

Much is made in my book about how the Islam bashers

and the Muslim terrorists legitimize each other. I came upon how both bashers and terrorists misrepresent the Koran in exactly the same ways. Simply put, they would misrepresent the Koran or leave parts of the Koran out of what they say, misquoting or leaving out exactly the same verses so as to support their positions. For example, they would agree that the Koran says "kill," one to use it to bash Islam and the other to justify their killing. But the Koran does not say "kill" as I will show. Both are wrong, both mislead.

The chapter *"The Koran Is Very Tolerant"* covers only the subject of tolerance, so greatly misunderstood in the West and also by those Muslims who attack community centers and the like. Muslim anti-this, anti-that rhetoric is so loud and widespread in the streets that it isn't surprising that ordinary Muslims don't bother to consult what the Koran actually says, not realizing that they are taking the risk that the street rhetoric misleads to their eternal disadvantage.

*"Islamic Law"* is the third chapter, describing one of the sources of the disconnect found between the Koran and how Islam is practiced by some believers. Man-made writings external to the divine Koran have been elevated in status by those with their own agendas and so challenge and contradict the divine Koran as being complete and fully explained in itself. Ordinary Muslims could be misled by all this or, unthinkingly, merely go along with it and not

4

realizing that the external writings could be straying if not contradicting the very words of God, which are in the Koran alone.

The following chapter *"Separation of Mosque & State, and Islam's Democratic Leanings"* picks up on the discussion of Islamic law and shows that the Koran supports community participation in government, actually presaging democracy while many Westerners and Muslims did not think that possible in Islam. The Koran recognizes and calls for secular society governed by the king's law, and seeks unity of the faithful only in matters of faith.

Having explained and proven though the use of references to the relevant Koranic verses what the Koran actually stands for, the next four chapters goes into the discussion of the sources and possible solutions to the disconnects between the Koran and how some believers actually practice Islam: *"Fundamentalism, Extremism & Terrorism," "The Ulama," "Fighting Back,"* and *"The Disconnect."* These chapters explain to Westerners what is going on in Islam that supplies fodder to the Islam bashers, and explains to ordinary Muslims how it seems to an outsider that they are being taken, being misled, and having their religion highjacked by the extremists.

The Appendix is in four parts, providing more detailed explanations of what had already been covered. The *"Advice to Would-Be Jihadists"* aims at countering suicide bomber recruiting efforts by emphasizing what the Koran says and pointing out how the potential recruits are being misled. *"Just & Unjust Jihads"* takes some ancient and recent wars involving Muslims and analyzes them in terms of the Koran and whether they could be considered just or unjust jihads. The role of the United States in the more recent wars is also discussed.

*"Responding to the Ayatollah Khomeini, Osama Bin-Laden & Hizbullah"* analyzes some extremist writings in terms of what the Koran actually says, pointing out how those writings misrepresent the Koran. *"A Brief History of Early Islam"* presents, in abbreviated form, the fascinating history of Islam from the time of Abraham and the Kaba.

Chapter One

# What The Koran Actually Says

Westerners tend to have misconceptions about what Islam stands for and what its divine Scripture, the Koran, actually says. This chapter corrects the misconceptions and provides other information that will allow readers to understand exactly what is in the Koran, and what it stands for and stands against.

Proof of what I say is provided by supporting quotes from the Koran. The "quotations" are shown here in bold, italicized print, and have been recast into modern English. They do not reflect the poetical beauty said to be in the original Arabic, but they do contain the gist (the essence and substance, and not the exact words) of what was written, and I used a number of different translations to make sure this is so. Translations of the Koran have proven to be perfectly fine. Since the different translations were invariably in substantive agreement, I knew I was getting accurate information.

The Koran happens to be very clear, surprisingly so for a Scripture. You will see that things are not a matter of interpretation and that the plain words of the Koran are clear enough. Those of the *ulama* (the learned ones) who chose to do so rely on the "interpretations" they make to suit themselves, or on blatant disregard of the Koranic text, and that underlies the disconnect between what the Koran stand for and the practice of those who so innovate on the Scripture.

Astoundingly, Western writers who bash Islam find support in the same omissions and "interpretations" the terrorists use. With the bashers and the terrorists saying the same thing, they legitimize each other. They effectively say that the other speaks the truth. Islam bashers will assert that the Koran says "kill," and the terrorists respond by saying that they agree, and they kill. But the Koran does not say "kill." Both the bashers and the terrorists find it useful to misrepresent the Koran to further their own purposes, leaving Westerners and ordinary Muslims sounding nonsensical when they say that Islam is really a religion of peace.

Let me explain Arabic term "*ulama*" for it is key to understand what is going on in Islam. Since ancient times, the *ulama* had been a lose community of the learned, the scholars, educators, jurists and others with knowledge. These were the educated, the respected, and presumably the wise. As with the learned anywhere, there was a diversity of opinion and a tendency to be of fixed opinion. Religion became a major area of interest and learning. Over time, some *ulama* aggregated religious authority to themselves and became what could be called clerics and act as such. They would be self-appointed in that the Koran appoints no religious hierarchy and appoints no intermediary between believers and "Allah" ("God" in Arabic).

This is in contrast to Christianity where the words of Jesus in the Gospels established a church and a religious hierarchy. Judaism also had a scripturally authorized priesthood, but that priesthood disappeared after the destruction of the Jerusalem Temple by the Romans. The rabbinate of Judaism, which sprung from the congregation leaders in the scripturally unauthorized synagogues, usurped religious authority like the *ulama* was later to do in Islam.

Most Westerners are accustomed to the existence of scripturally authorized clerics and would not question the authority of clerics of other religions, not realizing that Islamic clerics do not get their authority from a delegation in the Scripture of Islam, the Koran.

Each Muslim is to have his or her direct relationship to Allah. That requires a personal knowledge of the Koran, but unfortunately too many rely on their clerics and other learned men, a situation that is not dissimilar in other religions. Perhaps in the ancient days people took the time to learn what their Scriptures actually said and, as a result, followed them more closely. Today there is probably more empty repetition and recitation than independently pursued understanding.

## THE KORAN OVERRIDES EVERYTHING

My book focuses on the Koran alone, the only divine writing by Allah. I take the position that any writing in contradiction to the Koran must yield to the Koran because only the Koran is divine; and any writing that accords with the Koran is merely redundant. Thus, both conflict and agreement arising from any other source should be disregarded, and is disregarded in this book.

The Koran needs neither interpretation, nor interpretative help because it says so and also because its words are very clear. Those who dissemble say the Koran needs to be supplemented, as if Allah was not capable of saying what He meant. The matter is pointedly and directly addressed in the Koran itself:

*The Koran is a clear statement (3.138).*
*Allah has revealed the Koran to you explaining all things (16.89).*
*The Koran was sent to you explained in full detail (6.114).*
*Allah has expounded on everything with distinctive explanation (17.12).*

## KILLING ALLOWED ONLY IN SELF-DEFENSE

Portraying Islam as requiring violence is a ploy of the extremists amongst the *ulama* to help justify the violence they must use to further their causes. For instance, the Ayatollah Khomeini's admonishment (which is dissected in detail in the Appendix) includes the following statement:

Those who follow the rules of the Koran are aware that we have to kill. War is a blessing for the world and for every nation. It is Allah himself who commands men to wage war and to kill.

The Ayatollah makes it appear that Allah gives carte blanch authority to Muslims to go out and kill, or, worse, commands it. That is not what the Koran says. The Koran forbids Muslims to kill because Allah made all life sacred life. An exception is carved out allowing killing in self-defense when Muslims are attacked first, and that is the only exception:

*Whoever killed a human being (unless as punishment for murder or treason), it shall be as though he slew all mankind; and whoever saved a life, it shall be as though he saved all mankind (5.32).*

*You should not take life made sacred by Allah, except by way of Allah's law and justice (6.151).*

*Allah permits Muslins to fight if war is first made on them (22.39).*

*Fight in the way of Allah those who fight against you, but do not begin the hostilities. Allah does not love aggressors (2.190).*

The fact that Muslims are allowed to fight only in self defense is recognized by terrorists. That is shown by their striving to find or invent excuses as to how they have been attacked first. Building an airbase in Saudi Arabia with the permission of that Islamic government is deemed to be an attack, as is the existence and spread of Western culture and music. But the Koran refers to violent attacks, as was the case in the ancient agrarian society when Allah revealed the Koran to the Prophet Muhammad.

## MUSLIM ARE LIMITED TO RETALIATION IN-KIND

Nevertheless, whether the claimed attack is violent or non-violent, Muslims are limited to responding only in-kind. The Koran is explicit as can be in forbidding escalation:

*Give as you get; attack in the manner you were attacked (2.194).*

*When you retaliate, retaliate no worse than the fashion you were confronted with (16.126).*

There is no way for suicide bombing to comply with these Koranic verses as to retaliation only in-kind. Neither the terrorists nor the Islam bashers mention this. If a cultural attack is claimed, the only permitted response is a cultural response. The limitation to retaliation in-kind should be enough to counter the false claims dredged up by terrorists to cover their beginning of hostilities, and enough to show the Islam bashers that the Koran stands for peace.

## EVERONE BEARS ONLY THEIR OWN BURDENS

Jihadists actually destroy their chances of going to Paradise, not assure it as the firebrand clerics tell them. Although they might not be aware of it, the responsibility for determining whether the cause they have been sold is a just cause rests with the would-be jihadist:

*Whoever helps a good cause will have its reward and whoever helps an evil cause will bear the burdens of it (4.85).*

*If a person comes to you with a report, look carefully into the truth lest you harm someone unawares and afterwards be sorry for your actions (49.6).*

Being "sorry" means going to Hell. Islam stands for individual responsibility for one's own acts. Muslims are rewarded or punished only for what they themselves do on earth.

## THERE IS NO INHERITED SIN IN ISLAM, BUT MUSLIMS DO BEAR THE SINS OF THOSE THEY MISLEAD

The firebrand clerics also have something to worry about. There is an exception to bearing only your own burdens. The exception is not that the son bears the sins of the father or of past generations as some erroneously attribute to the Koran. There is no inherited sin in Islam. The only exception is that a Muslim will also bear the sins of the badly informed people they mislead:

*The ancient Jews and Christians have passed away and theirs is what they had earned, while their progeny earn what is theirs and are not to be asked what their ancestors did (2.141).*

*Everyone will bear their own evil burdens in full on the day of judgment, and also the evil burdens of any unknowledgeable people they misled (16.25).*

## THERE IS NO BEING "SAVED" IN ISLAM; ALLAH BALANCES A PERSON'S ENTIRE RECORD

On the day of judgment, Allah will have a person's entire record before Him. Nothing is omitted from that record. Nothing has been forgiven and no absolutions are to be offered. There is no salvation or being saved. Allah balances the good and the evil, taking both sides of the ledger into full account. Evil deeds can be offset by good deeds, and good deeds can be overwhelmed by evil deeds or even one evil deed. The balance is solely Allah's:

*On judgment day, the command judgment shall be entirely Allah's, and no person shall have power to do anything for another person (82.19).*

*Every man's actions will cling to his neck and Allah will bring his book of account wide open for him to see on the day of judgment (17.13-14).*

*Allah will justly balance a person's good and evil deeds so as to not wrong anyone in the slightest degree on the day of judgment (21.47).*

*If your scale is heavy with good deeds, you will be*

*successful on the day of judgment; if your scale is*
*light with good deeds, you will be ruined (7.8-9).*

## MUSLIMS CAN'T GET TO PARADISE BEFORE THE TRUMPETS ARE BLOWN ON JUDGMENT DAY

But the jihadist's greatest misimpression is probably that he would go to heaven and immediately wed one or more of the black-eyed virgins. That is the belief of the suicide bombers as shown in the videos they make of the ceremonies before the bombings.

The first error is that everyone, including jihadists, has to await the day of judgment called by Allah before anyone goes to Paradise. It has been over a thousand years since the advent of Islam, and Allah is yet to have a day of reckoning -- the trumpets haven't yet blown. Until that time, the jihadist will rot in his grave if he has one. When Allah calls the day of judgment, the living will be judged along with the dead as the earth will be no more as we know it. So leading a righteous life on earth does not delay anything, nor would committing suicide accelerate anything as all are judged at the same time:

*Every person will receive their reward only on the day of*
*judgment (3.185).*
*On the one day that all people come up pleading for*
*themselves, they will be fully compensated for their*
*actions and none will be treated unjustly (16.111).*
*Allah created man, made the way easy for him, caused*

*him to die, assigned a grave to him, and then, when Allah wills it, He raises him to life again (80.19-22).*
*When the trumpet is sounded, the dead will rise from their graves and hasten unto Allah (36.51).*
*When heaven bursts asunder and earth casts forth what is in it, those who strove hard for Allah will be joyful and the others will go into the burning fires of perdition (84.1-12).*

There are no exceptions in the Koran for a jihadist. The pattern is the same as in the other Abrahamic religions. Everyone must await the day of judgment announced by trumpets and unmistakable cataclysmic events before the Paradise or Heaven becomes available.

## PARADISE, AS DESCRIBED IN THE KORAN, IS ONLY A PARABLE

The Koranic description of Paradise is a parable, apparently meant to be only illustrative and not to be relied upon as such. The Prophet Muhammad is said to have confirmed this by pointing out that the blessings of Paradise cannot be conceived or known by man. Whatever Paradise is, it is not as it is on earth. The parable language is meant to convey that the Koran is only describing a possible likeness or similitude:

*This is a parable of Paradise as promised to those who keep their duty: therein rivers flow, fruits are perpetual and plenty, and there is shade (13.35).*

*This is a parable of Paradise promised to the dutiful: therein are rivers of water incorruptible, rivers of milk of unchanging taste; rivers of wine delicious to drinkers, and rivers of honey pure and clear (47.15).*

Thus, the Koran is clear that Paradise exists, but is described only as a parable. Muslims are being directly and pointedly told that the descriptions cannot be taken literally as some insist on doing. Muhammad's statement suggests that Allah took this path in His revelations because man's mind could not conceive of it however it could be described.

Taken literally, Muhammad's statement would suggest that nothing we know of on earth could be found in Paradise for then we could conceive of it. The Koran does not go so far and says only that its descriptions are parables.

## THERE IS NO SEXUAL INTERCOURSE IN THE HEREAFTER

That there is sex in Paradise may be the biggest misrepresentation of all. Nowhere in the Koran does it actually say there is sexual activity in Paradise, a telling omission because the Koran can be very explicit about sex. There is no sex in the Christian Heaven as indicated in the

Gospel of Matthew,[2] which has relevance to Islam because Allah considers the Gospel as His own revelation:

*Allah has revealed the Koran to you, and verifies that He also revealed the Torah and Gospel (3.3).*

*Allah revealed to you the Koran and verifies the previous Scriptures He revealed before it, and Allah stands guard over all of them (5.48).*

*Muslims believe in Allah and the revelations in the Koran and in the revelations to Abraham, Ishmael, Isaac, Jacob and the tribes of Israel, Moses, Jesus, and to all the other prophets, and do not distinguish between any of them (2.136).*

It is also difficult to conceive that the Koran, which is so conservative in sexual matters, would open the floodgates to sexual activity in Paradise. There is much to show the absence of the sexual activity expected by the jihadists. Also, women get equal treatment in Paradise, and the existence of comparable sexual activity for women would be unthinkable in Islam. If man cannot conceive what is in Paradise, as Muhammad had said, whatever it is in Paradise, it could not include sexual activity as known on earth. The matter is given fuller explanation in the Appendix *"Advice To Would-Be Jihadists."*

---

[2] "For in the resurrection they neither marry, nor are given in marriage, but are as the angels of God in heaven (Matthew 22.30)." Angels do not have sex.

## SUICIDE IS NOT IN THE WAY OF ALLAH

There is also the probability that committing suicide would itself bar a jihadist from Paradise. The prohibition on casting yourself into perdition or killing yourself could relate to matters other than suicide, but still the Koran shows that suicide is not consistent with Allah's life-scheme. Allah's plan is upset when the jihadist commits suicide, causes his or her own death, unless you say it was all predetermined. But even then, the person who takes his or life knows the time of death, and death does not come unawares which is contrary to Allah's wishes:

*Do not cast yourself into perdition (2.195).*
*Do not kill yourselves (4.29).*
*Allah gives life and causes death (53.44).*
*Allah created you from clay and then decreed a fixed lifespan for you (6.2).*
*Knowledge of your fixed time of death is only with Allah, and death shall come on you unawares (7.187).*

## MUSLIMS ARE OBLIGED TO SETTLE DIFFERENCES AMONGST THEMSELVES

The firebrand clerics are part of the *ulama*, and their voices appear strong because the rest of the *ulama* do not take up the cudgel. The Koran casts a duty on the silent *ulama* as well as on ordinary Muslims to involve themselves when believers quarrel. They must make peace between Muslims who quarrel. Furthermore, Allah requires that they do not accept defeat in their peacemaking efforts, because if they fail to make peace, they have an affirmative duty to fight the party that does wrong:

*All believers are brethren and you have a duty to make peace between your contending brethren (49.10).*

*If parties of believers quarrel, make peace between them with fairness and justice. If one party does wrong to the other, fight the one who does wrong until they obey Allah (49.9).*

This does not mean that Muslims must fight each time brother Muslims get into an argument, but they have a duty to try to make peace. However, they must choose the right side and actually join in the fight where two groups of Muslims, be they sects or political parties or the like, start to fight. Allah does not want them to sit around and await the outcome. Admittedly, it seems tough to insert oneself in a fight, but that is the way of Allah, most clearly expressed in His Koran.

## FORCE IS NOT TO BE USED IN RELIGIOUS CONVERSIONS, AND THE WORLD NEED NOT BE CONVERTED TO ISLAM

The history of ancient Islamic violence does not support the proposition that Islam fought in order to force conversions to Islam. Islam is a proselytizer, as are other religions. All send believers to the nations of the world with the aim and hope that they will convert some people to their religion.  Islam is no different in this regard.  But there is no desire that all nations adopt Islam, for Allah wants diversity in religion.  He said so:

*If Allah had so wanted, He could have made all mankind a single people (11.118).*

*Allah could have chosen to make all the peoples a single people, but made them as they are in order to try them as they vie with one another in good works (5.48).*

The Koran also shows that Allah provided for freedom of religion.  The Koran acknowledges that man is free to have another religion, free to accept or reject Islam:

*I have my religion and you have yours and we each have our own recompense (109.1-6).*

*God is our Lord and your Lord.  For us are our deeds and for you your deeds, and there is no argument between us, and God will eventually gather us together (42.15).*

*Allah has provided the truth and man is free to believe or disbelieve (18.29).*

*Allah has shown man the way to religion that he may accept or reject (76.3).*

In the Koran, Allah gets as specific as telling Muslims how proselytizing <u>is to be done</u>.  Beautiful preaching and gracious argument is the way.  And it gets even more specific as Allah also tells Muslims how proselytizing <u>is not to be done</u> -- force is not to be used:

*Invite all to the way of Allah using reason and beautiful preaching, and graciously convince them using your best approach (16.125).*

21

*There should be no compulsion in religion (2.256).*

Like other religions, Islam is to be spread by peaceful proselytizing.  However, also like other religions, some extremists zealously exceed the mandate.  The image of a warrior Arab holding the Koran in one hand and his sword in the other and demanding that the captive on his knees choose between them is not based on any precept of the Koran.  Actually, that would violate Allah's dictates:

*If the people of the Book and the unlearned people turn their backs on submitting to Islam, your duty is only to have delivered the message (3.20).*

*Allah requires that you respect, show kindness and deal justly with those who do not fight with you for religion or drive you from your homes (60.8).*

History shows that Arabs had initially looked upon Islam as a religion for Arabs, avoiding conversions for a hundred years before reluctantly accepting them.  Then some of the *ulama*, rulers and army commanders did spread the religion by using force in contravention of the Koran.


## JUSTICE IS A CENTRAL TENET OF ISLAM

Muslims are commanded by Allah to be just.  The concept of justice is repeated so many times in the Koran and worked into so many verses that it can be view as a central tenet of Islam.  Acting justly is even commanded even if it is against self-interest, parents, relatives or friends. Allah Himself is always just:

*Allah mandates justice (7.29).*

*Allah commands justice and doing good (16.90).*

*When you judge, you should judge with justice (4.58).*

*Speak with justice even against a near relative (6.152).*

*Stand fast for justice and as bearers of witness even against yourself, parents, relatives or friends, rich or poor (4.135).*

*Allah will be unjust to no one (18.49).*

*Allah wills no injustice to any creature of His (3.108).*

## THE KORAN IS MOST TOLERANT, PARTICULARLY OF JEWS AND CHRISTIANS

The Koran accepts the Torah of the Jews and the Gospel of the Christians, explaining that they are revelations of Allah (3.3, 5.48). In addition to the Scriptures, the Jewish and Christian prophets are recognized as legitimate prophets alongside Muhammad. Muslims, Jews and Christian (and Sabians) have the same one and only God. Because of this, Jews and Christians are considered "People of the Book," entitled to special, tolerant treatment by Muslims. Jews and Christians are not pagans, polytheists, idolaters, unbelievers or non-believers. Neither are the Sabians who are thought to be a semi-Christian sect from Babylonia. The Koran consistently treats Jews and Christians as "believers:"

*Muslims believe in Allah and the revelations in the Koran and in the revelations to Abraham, Ishmael, Isaac, Jacob and the tribes of Israel, Moses, Jesus, and all the other prophets, and do not distinguish between*

23

*any of them (2.136).*
*Muslims should not argue with people of the Book in other than helpful ways, except for those of them who do wrong, and tell them that we Muslims believe in the revelations to us and in the revelations to you, and that our God and your God is the same one God (29.46).*
*In a promise binding on Allah in the Torah, Gospel and Koran, Allah admits to Paradise believers who devote their persons and their property fighting in God's way (9.111).*

The bottom line in exhibiting Islam's tolerance to Jew and Christians is Allah's willingness to accept them into Paradise. To be sure, there is plenty in the Koran criticizing the ancient disobediences, the Golden Calf incident of the Jews being the prime example, but that isn't much different than the criticism contained in the Hebrew Bible/Old Testament for the same wrongdoing. But still, in the end God accepted His wayward children as a parent would accept wayward children after criticizing and spanking them. So too does the Koran and Allah.

As long as Allah accept Jews and Christians into Paradise, as He said He would if they otherwise qualify on the same terms as Muslims (belief in God and the Last Day and doing good), one cannot maintain that Islam is intolerant of them. Thus, a Muslim admitted to Paradise might find himself sitting next to Jew or Christian:
*Whoever believes in God and the Last Day and does good, whether he be Muslim, Jew, Christian or Sabian,*

*shall have their reward and should have no fear nor grieve on judgment day (2.62).*

More to the point is the declaration in the Koran that the transgressions of the ancient Jews and Christians will not be cast on their current day progeny. Yet, so much continues to be made of the ancient transgressions by those in the *ulama* who are anti-Jewish and anti-Christian even in the face of a clear Koranic declaration that their offspring have no responsibility for it. The Koranic position is consistent in that every person is responsible only for his or her own deeds and not those of anybody else (with the sole exception of having to bear the evil burdens of someone you misled (16.25)). There is just no inherited sin in Islam: *The ancient Jews and Christians have passed away and theirs is what they had earned, while their progeny earn what is theirs and are not to be asked what their ancestors did (2.141).*

## THE SHARIAH IS NOT THE DIVINE LAW OF ISLAM AS ONLY THE KORAN IS DIVINE

The Shariah is a body of secular law the *ulama* pushes modern Muslim states to adopt as their "holy" secular law. The bulk of the Shariah is man-made and not "holy" in the sense of being divine and emanating from God. Only the Koran emanates from God and is divine. Small parts of the Koran, those parts relating to matter that could be viewed as basically secular matters, were included with the words and deeds of the Prophet Muhammad (called the "hadiths") to make up the Shariah and that gives rise to the claim that it be called "holy."

The Prophet Muhammad was not a "lawmaker" so his words and deeds cannot be considered "law" as that term is generally used. Muhammad himself says he was just a warner and messenger. And Muhammad also said he was a mortal man, not divine. But, being an exemplary Muslim, Muhammad's personal words and deeds were powerful and influential. Those words and deeds are the basis of the Shariah and are advanced as "holy" law while Muhammad himself said the following:

*I [Muhammad] have no knowledge of the unseen, no abundance of wealth, and adversity can touch me. I am only a deliverer of warnings and bearer of good tidings to those who have faith (7.188).*

*I [Muhammad] don't have the treasures of Allah, don't know the unseen, and I'm not an angel. I follow only what is revealed to me (6.50).*

*I [Muhammad] wasn't the first messenger and I don't know what will be done with me or you. I follow only what is revealed to me, and I'm only a deliverer of warnings (46.9).*

*I [Muhammad] am only a mortal man, a messenger (17.93).*

Muhammad's hadiths were assembled from the oral recollections of the people as best as could be done by the various schools of jurisprudence working on it about two centuries or 10 generations after Muhammad's death. Each school made its own collection of hadiths. They combined their hadiths with under 100 verses from the Koran that represent secular type rules, like those covering inheritance. That became the Shariah, which was called "holy" law, with each school of jurisprudence having their own version. Eventually, only four schools became prominent and survived with their hadiths and their Shariah.

The schools of jurisprudence were part of the *ulama* and they passed down their Shariah to future generations, who tried to get Shariah adopted as the secular law of the Muslim countries they reside in.   Once adopted and imposed, Shariah has to be interpreted and the school naturally assumes the roles of interpreter and enforcer.

The adoption of Shariah by a Muslim nation to substitute for its modern secular law is a major event fought out politically.   Most Muslim nations have resisted this, obviously because it could lead to the conversion of their modern society to something like the Taliban had in Afghanistan, obliterating the normal differences between secular and religious society.

In contrast, the Koran recognizes that there are laws, secular laws, in addition to Allah's own laws. The Koran shows that Allah contemplates that the people will create their own secular governments, write their own secular laws and judge themselves under those laws. The Koran provides no support for Shariah law, nor for any group of *ulama* to assume any of the authority the Koran gives to the people themselves:

**Do not associate with Allah that for which He has given you no authority in His revelations (7.33).**

**Affairs should be decided by taking counsel amongst yourselves (42.38).**

**Allah commands you to turn over the duties of government to worthy people and, when you judge them, you should judge with justice (4.58).**

## THE KORAN ACCEPTS THE SEPARATION OF MOSQUE AND STATE, AND ALSO PRESAGES DEMOCRACY

The Koran provides for no religious hierarchy, nor any "church" as such in Islam. But the Koran clearly accepts the dichotomy between the religious and the secular.

Muslims are to form their own secular governments (4.58). The Koran might even have presaged democracy by its emphasis on taking counsel amongst yourselves (42.38), which means deciding by community consensus. Government though consultation seems to be the Koranic demand, not the adoption of secular law promulgated centuries ago and handed down for adoption intact with no give and take in the process. Once secular governance is established, the Koran calls for obedience to it:

**Obey Allah and those in authority among you (4.59).**

The Koran did not provide for a clergy but some of the *ulama* interposed one between ordinary Muslims and Allah. Having thus aggregated to themselves the control of the religious apparatus, those in the *ulama* needed only to add control of the secular to have complete domination of Muslim life. They don't have to win over the population but only convince them to adopt Shariah law, and then it would be only a matter of time before those in the *ulama* were in total control. Afghanistan (of Taliban days) and the Sudan show how a society operates under Shariah law. There is no requirement that Muslim nations adopt Shariah law, and few have. They have learned the lessons of history and now resist Shariah. Much more on this later.

## THE KORAN LARGELY PROVIDES EQUALITY FOR WOMEN

It is easy to criticize Islam for what it has not yet done with respect to giving complete equality to women, but few recognize that the Koran was very liberalizing for women when it was revealed by Allah. In those days, women participated in their society but had few rights.

The Koran recognized the spiritual equality of women. The Koran stopped the treatment of women as property, and gave them inheritance rights. A woman was given the right to choose what she wanted to work at and keep what she earned. Women were given the right to initiate a divorce, and the simple divorces used by their husbands were done away with. Women were given a right of support under the Koran, although that might have existed before the Koran was revealed:

*Believers, whether male or female, who do good deeds will be admitted to Paradise and treated equitably (4.124).*

*Both men and women can inherit the property of parents and near relatives (4.7).*

*Women are not inheritable nor may their dowry be taken back against their will (4.19).*

*Allah has given more to some of you, which you should not covet. Both men and women shall have the benefit of what they earn (4.32).*

*Women have rights against their husbands similar to the rights their husbands have against them, but men are a degree above women (2.228).*

*Men have the obligations to protect and maintain women because Allah has given them greater strength and wealth to support them (4.34).*

The Koran gave Muslim women more rights than they would have had under the Bible (Hebrew Bible/Old Testament) of Judaism and Christianity. Actually, one is hard pressed to find any women's rights in the Bible, except for the right of protection (which instead of being a woman's right can be viewed as men protecting their chattels). Arabs had also treated women as chattels, but the Koran changed this by giving the women rights, like the right of divorce, the right to inherit and the right to have separate property.

Yet it is curious how all three religions tended to reverse what was contained in their Scriptures. The oppressive discrimination against women in the Bible was reversed to the extent that there is now largely equality between men and women in modern Judaism and Christianity. And the equality presented in the Koran was reversed in some Muslim nations, courtesy of those of the *ulama* who oppress and discriminate against women.

Some of the *ulama* forced extremely restrictive dress codes as compared to the Koran's modest requirements. Women were not to show their "adornments," a term that the Koran does not define. However, the reference to children shows that it speaks of nakedness. Some of the *ulama* in some countries called for very restrictive dress even though Muhammad's wives provided no precedent for it. The only clear dress requirement in the Koran is that women should cover their bosoms. Added limitations seem contrary to the dictates of the Koran:

*Women should not display their naked adornments except to husbands, fathers, sons and sisters and children who know nothing about women's nakedness. Head-coverings could be used to cover their bosoms (24.31).*

*Do not associate with Allah that for which He has given you no authority in His revelations (7.33).*

*You should not forbid the good things which Allah has made lawful for believers (5.87).*

While women were given unprecedented rights in the

31

Koran, there was still some discrimination. Men were placed in charge of the affairs of women, perhaps flowing from having the obligation and duty to protect and support them (4.34). And men were to be a degree above women (2.228), perhaps because they had the right to rule the household. In some locations, female work options are limited although the Koran allows women to keep what they earn with mentioning any work limitations (4.32). Only men were given polygamous rights, while both men and women were required to act modestly:

*Marry even two, three or four woman if you feel that you can treat them justly (4.3)*
*Believing men and women should lower their gazes and act modestly (24.30-31).*

The Koran was like a breath of fresh air for women when it was revealed because Islam thereupon provided the best treatment of women. However, the liberality of the Koran was distorted and made restrictive by some of the *ulama* in some locations.


## NEITHER ADULTERERS NOR APOSTATES SHOULD BE KILLED ACCORDING TO THE KORAN

Islam is severe in its punishments as one could understand from the harsh desert environment it grew up in and the toughness of the desert people. Thieves were to be punished by mutilation, a Koranic injunction that is not even followed by extremists today. However, in other respects, the punishments of the Koran were significantly elevated by those in the *ulama* who desired it.

The Koran specifies whipping for adulterers; harsh as that seems as a punishment but consistent with its era. Whipping or flogging remained in use until relatively modern days, as shown by its use when British Men of War ruled the waves. Stoning to death for adultery was made up by someone in the *ulama* and is conspicuous absent in the Koranic verses dealing with adultery. The "holy" law of at least one Muslim nation specifies stoning.[3] It would seem that stoning would have been specified in the Koran instead of flogging if that had been Allah's intention:

***The man and woman guilty of adultery shall be flogged, each with a hundred stokes (24.2).***

Apostates are former believers who have left the religion. At times, they are derogatively called hypocrites. The Koran does not direct Muslims to kill apostates merely because they leave the religion. If the apostates conduct hostilities against believers, it becomes another matter. This is consistent with Koranic approach of permitting Muslims to kill only when they are attacked first:

***Apostates who turn to hostilities should be seized and slain wherever you find them (4.89).***

***Allah will not allow you to wage war against apostates***

---

[3] *Facing Death for Adultery [through stoning], Nigerian Woman Is Acquitted*, by Somini Sengupta, New York Times, September 26, 2003.

*who withdraw and do not fight you, offering you peace (4.90).*

Some in the *ulama* would have all apostates killed, meaning that nobody could ever leave the religion. That would destroy the religious freedom I have shown to exist in Islam (18.29, 76.3, 109.1-6) and also be in contravention of Allah's declaration that there should be no compulsion in religion (2.256). With people being free to accept or reject Islam, and with the use of force forbidden in getting people to join Islam, it is strange indeed for some of the *ulama* to call for death if someone leaves Islam.

Notwithstanding the clearly contrary language in the Koran, a few Muslim nations adopted the position of those *ulama* who forbad Muslims leaving the religion. However, those nations abandoned that position to conform to the United Nations Declaration of Human Rights adopted in 1948, which includes the freedom to change religious beliefs. Once again, those in the *ulama* had created a most negative view of Islam in clear contravention of the Koran, but other *ulama* thought better of it and removed the blot with the help of the United Nations position.

## ISLAM IS NOT DOUR

The Islam of the Arabs was a very simple and direct religion, a very sober religion, very human and very real, with the later converting Persians adding some embroidery and mysticism. The supernatural portrayed in the Koran is very limited. But Islam is not dour. The joy of life is there:

*You should not forbid the good things which Allah has made lawful for believers. (5.87).*
*Enjoy what you have lawfully won in war (8.69).*
*You should eat of the good things that Allah has provided for you (2.172).*
*Both men and women shall have the benefit of what they earn (4.32).*

Muslims are not to be jealous of one another, and should enjoy the benefits of what they earn. There is no prohibition against getting rich and enjoying one's wealth, but the rich should be more charitable. Muslims are not pushed to devote their entire lives to the religion:

*Allah has given more to some of you, which you should not covet (4.32).*
*The man with abundant means should spend abundantly, and the one of limited means spend what Allah has provided him (65.7).*
*Out of their love for Allah, the righteous give of their wealth to near kin, to orphans, to the needy, to wayfarers, to those who ask, and to set slaves free (2.177).*
*Pious monastic life is the innovation of others, not Allah. Allah requires only that believers please Him by right observance (57.27).*

The respect for poetry in the Koran, and the beautifully poetic way the Koran is said to be written, bespeaks of a society much broader than one of intertribal wars and highjacking caravans. In pre-Islamic days, tribes had charming poetical and oratorical battles, with one tribe challenging another to a contest of their best poets and orators, a tradition held in such high esteem that it deserved the name of *glorious* combat. Again, the reality is contrary to the popular belief about Islam.

Music was always a part of Islam; in some locations an important part. But some of the *ulama* made up rules against it. In some locations, music was barred it, but those *ulama* were not consistently successful because the Koran is not in the least adverse to music and music is popular in Muslim countries.

The Koran appears to take an ambivalent position concerning wine, first referring to it favorably and later unfavorably, but never specifically forbidding its use in non-intoxicating quantities. Wine remained included in the parable about Paradise (47.15). Where the conservative *ulama* are strong, wine is forbidden. If Islam is viewed as being dour, ascribe it to just some of those in the *ulama*, not to all of the *ulama*, not to ordinary Muslims and not to the Koran.

## ISLAM IS NOT A FAILED RELIGION, BUT IS TROUBLED ONE DUE TO THE *ULAMA*

An erroneous allegation by the Islam bashers is that

Islam is a failed religion by virtue of not having served its people well. The bashers point to the sufferings of Muslims in terms of their humiliations, anguish, and poverty. However, as a religion, Islam is a great success with one sixth of the world's population being believers. The shortcomings, in those locals where they do exist, appear to be mostly attributable to those in the *ulama* who put such a damper on Islam.

Their influence is most strongly exhibited by the influence they have on extremists or terrorists. The firebrands amongst the *ulama* provide the recruiting information or actually recruit jihadists for terrorist activities in contravention to the clear dictates of the Koran. Others amongst the *ulama* strive to get their Shariah adopted as a means to political power. Both serve to create disunity, strife, conflict and the concomitant drain on local society sapping the wealth and talent of the people.

They, not the ordinary Muslims, hold Muslim society back and provide the ammunition for the Islam bashers. It is almost as if the extremist *ulama* are working hand-in-hand with the Islam bashers as their positions so frequently coincide.

The Koran itself clearly stands for peace and Islam calls itself the "House of Peace," a take-off from the Koranic verse which states that Islam is the abode of peace: *Allah invites whom He will to the abode of peace, and guides those He pleases to the right path (10.25).*

Centuries ago, some member of the *ulama* took this and coined "House of War" as a label for lands outside of Islam. The Islam bashers make use of the inflammatory language as if it emanated from the Koran. Don't blame Islam, ordinary Muslims, or the Koran.

Chapter Two

# The Koran Is Very Tolerant

Islam is a most tolerant religion based on a fair reading of the Koran. I will prove this to you while taking note at the same time that the present day practice in Islam is to the contrary. The disconnect between the religion and the practice is most clearly illustrated when you focus on the relationship between Arabs and Jews.

Although the parties themselves might not care to acknowledge it, Arabs and Jews are brothers. Ishmael and Isaac were brothers, their father being the Patriarch Abraham. Ishmael begat the Muslims of Arabia, and Isaac begat the Jews of Canaan Palestine. The scientific record accords as both the Arabs and Jews are Semitic peoples.

Along with having originally sprung from the same gene pool, over the centuries the conversions of Jews and

Christians (many of whom were converted Jews) into Islam continued to nurture the same gene pool. Even the gates of ancient Jerusalem refers to the brotherhood of Ishmael and Isaac, carved in stone and recognized by all but today skirted by the parties themselves. Genetically, the Arabs are closer to Jews than the Arabs are to many of their Muslim brothers throughout the world.

While the Koran is tolerant to all, it is particularly tolerant to Jews and also to Christians. Yet the rhetoric on the street is anti-Jew. As one analyzes the Koran and Islamic history, it becomes obvious that the rhetoric has a political, not religious base. Politics are temporal, changing in time, while the religion as defined by the Koran is eternal, providing hope that Arabs and Jews will become brothers once again.

## ISLAM IS PARTIAL TO JEWS AND CHRISTIANS

Islam is not a religion opposed to Judaism and Christianity. The Koran accepts and builds upon Torah and Gospel, with the Koran being a continuation of them. In addition to honoring the Judaic and Christian Scriptures, the Jewish and Christian prophets are recognized as legitimate prophets alongside Muhammad. Muslims, Jews and Christians have and believe in the same God.

*Allah has revealed the Koran to you, and verifies that He also revealed the Torah and Gospel (3.3).*

*Allah revealed to you the Koran and verifies the previous Scriptures He revealed before it, and Allah stands guard over all of them (5.48).*

*Muslims believe in Allah and the revelations in the Koran and in the revelations to Abraham, Ishmael, Isaac, Jacob and the tribes of Israel, Moses, Jesus, and to all the other prophets, and do not distinguish between any of them (2.136).*

*Muslims should not argue with people of the Book in other than helpful ways, except for those of them who do wrong, and tell them that we Muslims believe in the revelations to us and in the revelations to you, and that our God and your God is the same one God (29.46).*

Because the Koran continues the revelations of Torah and Gospel, Jews and Christians were considered "People of the Book," entitled to special, tolerant treatment by Muslims. The Koran consistently treats Jews and Christians as believers; not disbelievers, not idolaters, not pagans and not polytheists. All places of worship, including churches and synagogues were protected by Muslims. Muslims could marry Jewish and Christian women, and could eat Jewish food:

*Allah could have chosen to make all the peoples a single people, but made them as they are in order to try them as they vie with one another in good works (5.48).*

*But for Allah's protection, monasteries, churches, synagogues and mosques where God's name is often mentioned would have been torn down (22.40).*

*It is lawful for Muslims to eat the food of Jews and*

*Christians and marry their chaste women (5.5).*

One of Muhammad's wife was Jewish, taken in battle after her husband and her father were slain. Her name was Safiyya and she was his 10<sup>th</sup> wife. With Muslims being permitted to marry Jewesses and with Muhammad himself having done so, it would appear difficult indeed to maintain that Muhammad or Islam was anti-Jewish.

Although Muslims have Koranic permission to eat both Jewish and Christian food, Christians do not today process their food as the Jews do, leaving only Jewish food as being okay for Muslims.

## JEWS AND CHRISTIANS CAN BE ADMITTED TO PARADISE

The possibility of being admitted into Paradise is very important to Muslims. It is the final reward and Allah alone makes that determination on judgment day (82.19) after consulting the book kept on each person (17.13-14). Allah sits in judgment of Jews and Christians who might also be admitted to Paradise in addition to Muslims. The requirements for Jews and Christians to be admitted are the same as for Muslims. Thus, a Muslim might earn a reward in Paradise and find Jews and Christian there:

*In a promise binding on Allah in the Torah, Gospel and Koran, Allah admits to Paradise believers who devote their persons and their property fighting in God's way (9.111).*

*Whoever believes in God and the Last Day and does good, whether he be Muslim, Jew, Christian or Sabian, shall have their reward and should have no fear nor grieve on judgment day (2.62).*

*God is our Lord and your Lord. For us are our deeds and for you your deeds, and there is no argument between us, and God will eventually gather us together (42.15).*

This alone belies the rhetoric heard against Jews and Christians. No matter what criticism has been levied against Jews and Christians, in the end they are treated the same way Muslims are treated. Paradise is the final reward and is of the upmost importance. All else is rendered insignificant and brushed aside in this ultimate benevolence to Jews and Christians.

## THE KORAN JUDGES ON AN INDIVIDUAL BASIS, FORBIDDING GROUP CONDEMNATION

Islam requires that individuals must be judged independently as individuals based on what they individually have done, and not judged on the basis that they are part of a group. An individual cannot carry any burden the individual does not personally create. What I have called an exception, of also carrying the burden of people they misled, is not truly an exception because the individual personally acted to mislead and thus personally created the burden to be borne. In Islam is there no carry-over or transference of a burden or sin from father to son, or from an ancestor to descendent, or in any other way. Nor can a burden carry-over from a group, whether a living or ancient group, to an individual. Group condemnations are forbidden:

*Whoever helps a good cause will have its reward and whoever helps an evil cause will bear the burdens of it (4.85)*

*Everyone will bear their own evil burdens in full on the day of judgment, and also the evil burdens of any unknowledgeable people they misled(16.25).*

*People of a group are not all alike. There are those amongst the People of Book who are upright, believe in God and the Last Day and recite His messages throughout the night; they are righteous and their good deeds will not be denied them (3.113-5).*

*There are good people amongst the Jews who speak the truth and do justice with it (7.159).*

*The ancient Jews and Christians have passed away and theirs is what they had earned, while their progeny earn what is theirs and are not to be asked what their ancestors did (2.141).*

Yet there are parts of the Koran that criticize the ancient Jews and Christians. These are the focus of those Muslims who chose to be anti-Jewish, anti-Christian, anti-American (America being the proxy for Christians and/or Crusaders) or even anti-Semitic, which is inexplicable as Arabs are also Semites. This is the manna of the extremist *ulama* but the Koran provides no justification for group condemnation.  God's creatures may have strayed as in the Golden Calf incident, and the One God already punished them.  In the end, He still accepts them as His children and judges them individually, and will admit them to Paradise if individually deserving.  That is exactly what He will do with Muslims.

## THE KORAN'S TOLERANCE GOES FURTHER, BLENDING INTO KINDNESS

By now it should be clear that the Koran does stand for peace and tolerance notwithstanding the disconnects in practice by some Muslims.  Allah commanded religious freedom and shunning the use of force in religion.  Allah commanded Muslims not to fight and kill unless attacked first, and then commanded them not to escalate the fighting.  Allah wanted a diversity of peoples and allowed Muslims to live in peace with those others, carving out a special position for Jews and Christians by treating them as believers entitled to go to Paradise.

And the Koran goes further, mandating that Muslims be kind to the "other" and treat them with respect.  Also Muslims are commanded to not react negatively to rejection. The Koranic moral standard is high:

*If the people of the Book and the unlearned people turn their backs on submitting to Islam, your duty is only to have delivered the message (3.20).*
*Believers should forgive those who do not believe (45.14).*

*Allah requires that you respect, show kindness and deal justly with those who do not fight with you for religion or drive you from your homes (60.8).*

## THE TOLERANCE OF MUHAMMAD

The early wars of Islam were political actions, as was Muhammad's clashes with the three rebellious Jewish tribes. However, the extremist *ulama* seize upon the clashes with the Jewish tribes to mislead Muslims into disobeying the Koranic directive to be tolerant, specifically of Jews.

Muhammad fled Mecca in 622 because he lost the protection of his family and his life was placed in danger. He had an invitation from Medina to become its political leader and he accepted it. The Medina tribes felt they needed an outsider to settle the intertribal. conflicts that could lead to civil war. Three Jewish tribes were part of those who extended the invitation to Muhammad.

The gesture was obviously political, not religious, as the invitation was extended by Jews and other tribes that were neither Jewish nor Muslim. At that time, there were no Muslims in Medina. It cannot be said that the Medina invitation was an invitation to become the religious leader of Medina.

In those days, intertribal fighting was the norm, not the

exception. The weak tribes allied themselves with protectors giving them security, but as one group or another started to have too much influence or strength, or too little, wars started. In Medina, Muhammad coalesced the different factions including the Jewish tribes. He established himself as the political leader of the community, but not the religious leader of Medina as Islam was not then generally accepted and there were still few believers in Medina.

In Islam's first major battle two years later in 624 at a location called Badr, the most important battle of Islam, Muslims made up only fraction of Muhammad's fighting force, maybe a fifth. The Jewish tribes contributed their share and fought alongside the first Muslims.

Stories abound about what actually happened in that era since there wasn't much being written. Nevertheless, it was said that as Muhammad became stronger, the balance of power in Arabia changed and alliances shifted politically. None of the history indicates any anti-Jewish bias in Arabia other than the normal political rivalry between tribes and the new concern that Mohammad was getting too strong politically.

The three Jewish tribes were sent away from the Medina area by Mohammad in 625 for fomenting political dissension, as was the political way in those days of handling dissension and consistent with the Muslim religious belief that Muslims should not kill unless attacked first. Later, in 627, one of the Jewish tribes joined the Meccan army in the "trench" war that Muhammad won, and the men of that tribe were slaughtered the women and children taken as slaves.

Muhammad's 10th wife was Jewish, taken in battle after her husband and her father were slain in a battle. Her name was Safiyya. The Koran permits Muslim men to marry Jewesses and Muhammad did so, showing that Muhammad did not harbor any animosity toward Jews or Judaism.

## THE ADVENT OF POLITICAL ANIMOSITY

Nonetheless, the story of the three Jewish tribes was embellished by the anti-Jewish segment of the *ulama* and is misrepresented today by extremists so as to support their rhetoric against Jews. This is in conflict with the Koran and also with Western historians who invariably maintain that relationships with the Jews were very good in those ancient days. And, as should be noted, Muslim Baghdad had welcomed over a million Jewish residents knowing well the history of Islam. With some *ulama* being vociferously anti- Jewish, or really anti-Israel, Muslim historians are yet to be heard from.

Historians point to anti-Semitism as having a Christian

origin. In the Crusades, the Christian Crusaders killed Muslim and Jew indiscriminately, as Islam had always made a home for Jews in accordance with the Koran. Opposition to Jews arose only after 1948 when the State of Israel was created and the extremists in the Palestine *ulama* rejected the United Nations offer to create a sister Muslim state.

The ancient Islamic contacts with both Jews and Christians were extensive, perhaps numerically more with the Christians who had the greater population. And perhaps for the same reason, there were more wars with Christianity. The Jews were never a danger to Islam, either theologically or practically. Animosity toward Jews did not first arise in Islam; it arose in Christianity along with animosity toward Muslims. The Crusades showed that Muslims and Jews were on equal footing in the eyes of Christianity. Christianity became Islam's foe, not Judaism. Islam's greatest triumphs are said to be the capture of Constantinople and the defeat of the Crusaders, not the capture of Jerusalem nor the building of the Dome of the Rock in Jerusalem.

In addition, the similarities between Judaism and Islam are striking. Judaism and Islam arose directly from Abraham and are named after his sons. Neither Judaism nor Islam has a scripturally mandated religious hierarchy. The imamate of Islam is similar to the rabbinate of Judaism and neither is a required intermediary to God. The system of issuing rulings is the same in Judaism and Islam; *responsa* by the rabbis and *fatwa* by the imams. Jewish law is similar to Islamic law. The Jewish food laws, and in particular the rituals connected with animal slaughter, are close and Muslims may eat Jewish food.

There is just no Koranic support for those in the *ulama* who conduct the vendetta against Jews and Judaism. Nor can such *ulama* find any anti-Jewish support in the historical relationship between Muslims and Jews or in Muhammad's life.

## THE STATE OF ISRAEL

The vendetta against Jews is of very recent origin, having support in neither the Koran, nor Islamic history, nor in Muhammad's life. The vendetta is less than a century old. It arose only when the State of Israel was created in 1948 and is clearly of political origin. Had that land been given to someone else, the extremist response would undoubtedly have been the same -- highlighting that the matter was political and not religious.

The British had their Balfour Declaration promising the Jews a state as far back at 1917, but nothing came of that until Hitler's pogroms against Jews created an Jewish exodus to Palestine that had to be addressed. It was addressed by the United Nations creating the State of Israel in 1948 out of the British mandate of Transjorden, which was under the sovereignty of the Hashemite dynasty that once vied for control of Mecca. In the intervening years following the Balfour Declaration, extremist Muslims romanced Hitler and flirted with Nazism. It was not a matter of religion; it was practical politics.

At the time Israel was established, the extremist *ulama* didn't even have anti-Jewish rhetoric they could use. Although Islam had a thousand year history of the most diverse religious scholarship, only one exception could be found exhibiting an anti-Jewish bent. That was in the writings of Ibn Hazm (994 – 1064 CE), a great poet and author, and hater of both Jews and Muslim Shiites -- indicating that something other than religion was at work in him. Islam had no significant body of written material attacking Judaism and Jews. Nazi literature was imported, and the extremist *ulama* started to write.

When Israeli statehood was in the works, Palestinians felt they could live and work with the Jews in the new state. The Palestinian press at that time reflected this view for all to see. But a few extremists in the *ulama* would not let this happen and they fomented discord. The United Nations responded by offering to carve out a separate state for the Palestinians. The offer was rejected by the Imam of Jerusalem, a most extreme member of the *ulama* and the man most responsible for romancing Hitler.

The ordinary Palestinians Muslims never got to vote, a situation that continues to this day as the extremist *ulama* perpetuates their opposition to the Jewish state. But there was an exception as moderate Muslims recently got their own voice, so long denied to them by the extremists.

If one looks at the history of Islam and the history of the extremist *ulama*, one starts to wonder whether the extremist's primary concern was the secular Jewish State of Israel or the prevention of still another secular Muslim state in Islam, this one in Palestine. That is, the true enemy of the extremist *ulama* may well be the secular Muslim society and not Jews and not the State of Israel. If this be so, the corollary would be that the true enemy of the Palestinian Muslims is their own extremist *ulama*, not the Jews or Israel.

Getting back to the Koran, Islam gets high marks on tolerance. Islam was most tolerant of Jews and Christians until the politics of the Middle East interfered. The spoiler was and remains the extremist *ulama*, and possibly also the moderate *ulama* who fail in their Koranic duty to counter the extremists:

*All believers are brethren and you have a duty to make peace between your contending brethren (49.10).*
*If parties of believers quarrel, make peace between them with fairness and justice. If one party does wrong to the other, fight the one who does wrong until they obey Allah (49.9).*

## THE TOLERANT NATURE OF ISLAM'S *DHIMMA* ARRANGEMENTS

*Dhimma* (minority) treatment of captive peoples has been criticized by Western authors as making the captives second-class citizens, as being discriminatory and as exhibiting Islamic intolerance. They are mistaken in their criticism.

*Dhimma* treatment originated after the death of Muhammad and before the Koran was compiled 20 years later. Circumstances suggested it when the Arab armies went beyond the Arabian Peninsula in their phenomenal record of military victories. In those formative years, many of the Arabian tribes joining Muhammad did so only for booty, not for the religion. They weren't yet Muslims. Muhammad's generals were Muslims, undoubtedly aware of the strictures not to kill unless attacked first, but had to continue the wars for booty and domination, then the way of the world.

Victory gave them the sought for booty and the option of killing their captives, enslaving them, or letting them live and exacting an annual tribute. Their choice was the latter, a clever choice in that it provided continuing benefit and allowed the Muslims to follow their embryo religion in stopping fighting when the enemy yielded. They knew the recitals of Muhammad which were later reflected in the final Koran:

*Desist from fighting the enemy if the enemy desists,
return to fighting if the enemy returns to the attack
(8.19).*
*Fight the enemy until there is no more disorder and the
peaceful ideals of religion prevail. But if they cease
fighting against you before then, stop hostilities
except against wrongdoers (2.193).*
*If the enemy is inclined to peace, you should also be
inclined towards peace (8.61).*

The decency of *dhimma* treatment becomes apparent
when contrasted to the usual killing or enslavement of
captured peoples in ancient days. Killing and enslavement
was the standard practice until Islam came along and
developed *dhimma* treatment for captured people. While
wars for booty and domination are to be condemned,
*dhimma* treatment is to be applauded.

*Dhimma* treatment allowed the captured peoples live
and to continue practicing their religion. At that time this
largess was not so much a reflection of Muslims being
forbidden to force conversions to Islam (later appearing in
the Koran as 2.256) as it was the belief that Islam was a
religion for Arabs, revealed by Allah for Arabs. Arab
garrisons were built out of town so as to avoid mixing with
the local people and to keep by themselves in their religion.
Later, when the Arabs got their own Scripture, the Koran,
they must have felt better about being on a par with the
Jews and Christians who had their own Scriptures, but
viewing Islam as an Arab religion prevailed for a century or

more.

The *dhimma* approach was said to have been developed by the Caliph Umar, who started his reign two years after the death of Muhammad, although there are indications that some sort of predecessor arrangements had existed in Arabia. Umar started his reign as caliph two years after Muhammad's death at which time the Arabian Peninsula was largely conquered and subdued. Umar needed to conduct wars for booty outside of Arabia so as to keep his troops together.

He invaded northern areas where more Jews, Christians and others minorities were located. Heretofore, in Arabia, these groups lived amongst Arabs in cities like Mecca, or by themselves in remote areas like Medina. These relatively small tribes banded together with Arab tribes for mutual protection, as exhibited by the three Jewish tribes of the Medina area inviting Muhammad to make peace in Medina and become its secular leader.

Umar faced much larger tribes in the North. He formalized the arrangements with the newly conquered in what might be considered to be a contract. In agreeing to these *dhimma* arrangements, the *dhimmi* people acknowledged their subservience to Muslims, agreed to behave in certain ways, agreed to certain restrictions on their activities and in the number and size of their religious buildings, and agreed to pay an annual tribute or a poll tax.

In exchange, they were permitted to live their lives as they would, practice their religions and use their languages, and be entitled to security in their lives and possessions.

The new *dhimma* treatment was vastly different that what previously prevailed with minority people. Using the three Jewish tribes of Medina as an example, the trade-off become obvious. The Jewish tribes were full members of their communities, paying no special taxes and having to participate in wars. The *dhimmi* had to acknowledge their subservience, pay a special tax, agree to some restrictions on their activities, but were relieved from fighting. Both the old and new arrangements were tolerant, but the new *dhimma* arrangements clearly showed who the boss was.

The Muslims didn't need the *dhimmi* in their armies and probably didn't want them there. The Muslims were doing just fine and the conquered peoples weren't the best of fighters, a conclusion one might reach based on their being conquered. There may have also been uncertainly as to whether the *dhimmi* could be trusted in battle.

The *dhimmi* were probably happy not to have to fight. The *dhimma* arrangement was practical and brilliant in its appropriateness at that time and place. It wasn't a religious matter and the Muslims had no problem with granting the *dhimmi* religious freedom.

At that time, Muslims didn't want to convert others

and they didn't need that many slaves. They were astute and realized that a constant stream of poll taxes meant more over time than killing everyone, taking everything and moving on.

Today, Muslims are either criticized or applauded for their ancient *dhimma* arrangements. They might be criticized, as the Islam bashers do, for creating second-class citizens, even though citizenship wasn't much of a concept back then. The Muslims might also be accused of acting like extortionists offering protection for money, or like mercenaries, fighting for money. The Muslims could be accused of being segregationists or apartheids, although it seemed that some *dhimma* (particularly the Jews and Christians) were free to mix and intermarry. And, of course, there were Arab abuses from time to time, individual actions, macho stuff and things like that, something that might be expected in any society, but fertile ground for criticism by Islam bashers.

The better view is that the *dhimmi* paid tribute as a substitute for the tax Muslims have to pay pursuant to the Koran (the *zagat*) and as a contribution to the cost of protection. They were second class citizens in many ways, but didn't have to fight, which might be viewed as an offsetting advantage in an age when warfare was commonplace and killing or enslaving captured peoples was the standard practice.

Later, nearly a thousand years later, when the Ottoman raised the *dhimmi* to first class citizen status ostensibly for humanistic reasons and did away with the *dhimma* system, the *dhimmi* appreciated not paying the tribute but didn't at all like being drafted into the Ottoman military and fighting the Christian West. All in all, *dhimma* status wasn't all that bad -- and it was undeniably much better than being killed or enslaved when captured. The *dhimma* arrangements should not be viewed as a sign of Islamic intolerance for it was hardly that.

## THE KORAN DOES NOT AUTHORIZE KILLING "INFIDELS"

Islam has falsely been accused of killing "infidels" on sight and for no reason other than they are not Muslims. To be sure, some extremists have done so over the centuries but permission for it is not to be found in the Koran. It is contrary to the Koran. Killing without being attacked first is contrary to the way of Allah as expressed many times over in the Koran.

In Western usage, "infidel" is a loose and vague term essentially meaning the "other." The dictionary defines infidel in terms of a person who does not accept a particular religion. It can be a person who accepts no religion (an atheist) as well as a person who has another religion.

The word "infidel" not found in the Koran. The most widely used religious distinction found in the Koran is between a "believer" and a "non-believer" and in this distinction we immediately find the unexpected. The term "believer" does not only refer to Muslims but also covers, encompasses and includes Jews and Christians. The non-believers thus become the "other" under the Koran. Neither Muslim, Jew nor Christian can be considered "non-believers" under the Koran.

The term "idolater" is found in the Koran, a term having largely the same meaning as a "non-believer." "Idolater" refers to a worshipper of idols, which is forbidden under the Ten Commandments of the Torah (Hebrew Bible/Old Testament) and thus forbidden by the Koran. As a result, neither Muslim, Jew nor Christian can be treated as "idolaters" under the Koran since idols are forbidden to them. That is, an idolater has to be someone other than a Muslim, Jew or Christian. So too, the terms "pagan" or "polytheist" which are also found in the Koran. Muslims, Jews and Christians are not pagans or polytheists.

As previously expressed, the Koran is very consistent in allowing killing only when Muslims are attacked first. Even in the case of the disliked apostates (hypocrites who have left the religion), the Koran requires that they be left in peace if they do not attack first. To be sure, the Koranic mandate is to strive hard to bring apostates back into the religion, as it is to proselytize to other non-believers, but always without the use of force.

Rather than kill the non-believer, whether he or she be called an infidel, idolater, pagan or polytheist, the Koran consistently requires acceptance and even kindly treatment. The disconnect between what the Koran says and the "kill the infidel" mindset can be attributed to the *ulama* extremists or to zealots who do not understand or chose not to honor the Koran.

Chapter Three

# Islamic Law

The word "holy," which is clearly defined only in a dictionary, is applied to Islamic Law in many ways by many different groups. It seems far less controversial to just distinguish divine law from man-made law, and leave the word "holy" out of the discussion. The divine emanates from Allah alone, consisting only of the Koran and the old Scriptures (the Torah and Gospel) that Allah also revealed.

The components of what might be or has been considered Islamic law are discussed in this chapter. Starting with the Koran, the discussion turns to the "king's law" (secular law), followed by the "hadiths" (the words and deeds of Muhammad) and the Shariah (a combination of the hadiths and little of the Koran).

The commentary of scholars over the centuries is then addressed as is the curious use of rulings (*fatwa*) issued by individuals. The chapter closes with a discussion of Islamic attempts at law codification.

# The Divine Law of Islam

The divine law of Islam is the Koran, supplemented as it turns out by the old Scriptures (the Torah and Gospel) that Allah verified He wrote and still guards. Only Allah is divine, and the Koran, Torah and Gospel are His laws.

## REVELATION OF THE KORAN, BIRTH OF ISLAM

Islam was born in the 7th century in terms of the Gregorian or Christian calendar used in the West. That calendar dates from the time of Jesus, while the Islamic calendar starts with the date of the Prophet Muhammad's 200-mile pilgrimage *(hijra)* to Medina from his birthplace in Mecca. That was year 1 in the Islamic calendar, or year 622 in the Gregorian calendar. The *hijra* took place when Muhammad was forced to leave Mecca due to widespread opposition to the developing faith.

In the year 610, when Muhammad was a about 40 years old, he started receiving revelations from Allah and that continued until just before his death in 632. In Islam, age 40 is considered the age of spiritual maturity. The Koran was revealed piecemeal by Allah in Arabic to Muhammad through the voice of the angle Gabriel during this 22 year period:

*When man reaches forty years of age, he starts to give*

*thanks to Allah (46.15).*
*The Koran is a revelation from Allah, brought by the*
    *Faithful Spirit [the angel Gabriel] in plain Arabic*
    *(26.192-5).*
*Muhammad is the messenger of Allah and the last of  the*
    *prophets (33.40).*
*The Koran was not revealed all at once, and Allah*
    *arranged for it to be in the right order (25.32).*

While the Koran provides a clear explanation as to its
revelation by Allah, little light is cast on the human
compilation of those revelations into the final Koran, the
Book.  The final Koran contains over 6,000 verses arranged
in 114 chapters *(surahs)* of widely varying length.  It is
doubted that Muhammad himself recorded the revelations
in writing, but it is clear that Muhammad recited them out
loud as they were revealed to him:

*Abraham and Ishmael petitioned Allah to raise up a*
    *messenger from among the people who shall recite*
    *the messages of Allah to the people and instruct them*
    *in Scripture and wisdom (2.129).*

The references to "wisdom" in the Koran could not
have been references to the hadiths nor would it presage the
hadiths assembled some 200 years after the death of
Muhammad.  While Muhammad was an exemplary Muslim
and what he did and said would set a good example, the
Koran never elevated Muhammad's words and deeds
(hadiths) to laws that must be followed.  There is no grant
of authority in the Koran to Muhammad as a lawmaker but
only as a messenger and role model:

*The messenger of Allah [Muhammad] is an excellent exemplar for those who follow and praise Allah (33.21).*

The verses of the Koran itself are called the Book of Wisdom. Allah forbids anyone to add or subtract from His revelations in the Koran as the Koran explains everything and is complete:

*Allah has revealed the Koran to you, explaining all things (16.89).*

*The Koran was sent to you explained in full detail (6.114).*

*Do not associate with Allah that for which He has given you no authority in His revelations (7.33).*

*These, the verses of the Koran, are the verses of the Book of Wisdom (10.1).*

*This is the Book of Wisdom, its verses a guide and mercy for the doers of good who establish regular prayer, offer regular charity and are certain of the Hereafter (31.2-4).*

## COMPILATION AND PUBLICATION OF THE KORAN

There could have been scribes sitting at Muhammad's feet as he recited the revelations aloud, or those who heard the recitals could have later repeated them to scribes. In those days, there was no writing paper. Writings were on parchment, leather, sheep collarbones, camel bones, and palm-stems. The use of tablets of stone was possible, but doubted. There are Koranic references to ink, pens, and scribes.

In one way or another, the revelations got to those who later compiled the Koran. The surviving writings supplied some content, but most likely the bulk came from those persons who heard Muhammad's recitals and survived the subsequent wars. About two decades passed before Koran was compiled and published.

Over 6,000 verses had to be collected, put into order, and the Koran completed. The survivors who heard Muhammad recite had to be located and interviewed, their recollections reconciled and supplemented by whatever writings that could be found. It must have been a huge undertaking by the learned men who did the job, for the job was likely to have been entrusted to no-one else.

It was said that Umar, the caliph who ruled from 634 to 644 and completed the conquest of Arabia, started the collection process. Uthman, the caliph who ruled until 656, finished the compilation in about 652 or some twenty years after Muhammad's death.

Uthman was said to have burned all the materials and prior drafts that existed when the compilation was completed. Scribes then made copies for distribution, assuring that there would be only one version in existence. In all, from the commencement of the revelations to the completed and final Koran about 42 years passed.

The arrangement of the chapters (*surahs*) in the Koran

appears to be in the order of descending length. There is no indication how the verses were arranged within each chapter, except that it was done with divine guidance (25.32).

While it is clear that the Koran in use today is the same as the one completed under Caliph Uthman, no bits and pieces of the original writings have been found in any relic collection that would scientifically confirm anything about the compilation process and lay to rest any questions as to reliability. The most outlandish assertion is that the entire Koran was devised and written some time after the early Arab military conquests when Umar felt some religious glue was necessary for the troops before they moved out of Arabia. But the Koran is the Scripture of Islam and accepted and honored by all Muslims being the divine source of their religion:

*This day Allah perfected your religion for you and completed His favor to you by choosing Islam as your religion (5.3).*

*Allah has chosen you for His religion and has named you Muslims (22.78).*

## RELATIONSHIP OF THE KORAN TO THE JEWISH AND CHRISTIAN SCRIPTURES

The Koran took its place in a continuum of Scriptures. While Allah did clearly and directly state that Muhammad was the last of the prophets (33.40), He did not so say that the Koran was the last of His revelations. But Allah did say that the Koran was not the first of His revelations. The Koran follows and incorporates the Torah and the Gospel:

*Allah has revealed the Koran to you, and verifies that He also revealed the Torah and Gospel (3.3).*

*Allah revealed to you the Koran and verifies the previous Scriptures He revealed before it, and Allah stands guard over all of them (5.48).*

Thus, the Koran should be, or must be, read within the context of the Torah and Gospel as Allah revealed them all. This makes the Torah and the Gospel part of Islam, which Muslims implicitly recognize when they refer to the Creation narrative or other narratives in the Torah or the Gospel. All these Scriptures are thus considered divine in Islam, although they were written and compiled in different ways. They all emanated from the same One God:

*Muslims believe in Allah and the revelations in the Koran and in the revelations to Abraham, Ishmael, Isaac, Jacob and the tribes of Israel, Moses, Jesus, and to all the other prophets, and do not distinguish between any of them (2.136).*

*[W]e Muslims believe in the revelations to us and in the revelations to you, and that our God and your God is the same one God (29.46).*

The Koran contains the direct revelations of Allah, the very words of Allah delivered through repetition by an angel (Gabriel) and Muhammad. Those revelations were eventually reduced to writing and complied in the Koran, by human hands and thus subject to the normal range of human error. Unless it is said that all the humans were inspired and could make no errors, some errors might have crept into the process; and if they did we will never know for certain.

The direct revelation of the Koran is to be contrasted to the "indirect" revelation of the old Scriptures. Neither the "Bible" nor the "Christian Bible" contain the exact words of God uttered by God, but instead are the writings of human authors inspired by God. That inspiration gives those writings a divine source, but only the Koran has the actual words of God.

I should explain that the "Bible" is the Hebrew Bible of Judaism and the Old Testament of Christianity, the two being essentially identical (and are treated here as being one and the same). I use the term "Christian Bible" to encompass the Old Testament and the New Testament, the latter includes the four Gospels of Matthew, Luke, Mark and John, the epistles written by Paul, the Book of Revelations and other books.

You can see from this that the Koranic reference to the Torah and Gospel does not clearly relate to these old Scriptures as such. The Torah is the first five books of the Hebrew Bible/Old Testament which consists of some 39 books depending on how one counts them. The Torah is roughly one quarter the size of the entire Hebrew Bible but is considered the core of Judaism.

It is the Torah and not the complete Hebrew Bible that is likely to be found in most Jewish homes today, and that might have also been the case at the time Islam was born considering the size differential, the scarcity of materials and everything having to be hand written. For all we know, the word "Torah" used by the compilers of the Koran could have been meant to cover the entire Hebrew Bible. For example, this would be suggested by the Koranic reference to King David (say in 38.20) because King David is not mentioned in the Torah. He first appears on the scene in later books of the Hebrew Bible.

What the compilers of the Koran meant in their use of the word "Gospel" cannot easily be worked out. "Gospel" is in the singular while the New Testament contains four inspired Gospels. Still more gospels were excluded when the New Testament was compiled. The authors of the four Gospels were there to see and hear Jesus, and their Gospels give testimony as to that.

The Koranic reference to "Gospel" might have been aimed at the testimony about Jesus as a prophet of Allah with the focus being on the words of Jesus himself as contained in any one of or all of the Gospels. If that is the meaning of the compilers of the Koran, the epistles of Paul and the other books of the New Testament were meant to be excluded.

While Allah revealed, verified and continues to stand

guardian over the Torah and Gospel, Allah states that He might abrogate or change parts of them, substituting something similar or better. Whether Allah had done so, and the extent thereof, would be determinable from the substitutions that necessarily accompany the change. Two views of the same subject matter in the Koran and the old Scriptures could indicate the existence of a substitution. It would appear that old revelations wouldn't merely be dropped without bringing another:

*Whatever revelation Allah abrogates or causes to be disregarded in the old Scriptures, Allah brings one like it or better (2.106).*

Thus the Koran is the divine law of Islam supplemented by the Torah and Gospel except where abrogated. Where a revelation is found in the Torah or Gospel and the subject matter is not specifically addressed in the Koran or a substitution noted, that revelation stands. Thus, for example, the Ten Commandments of the Book of Exodus of the Torah would be part of the divine law of Islam. And so too Jesus' Sermon on the Mount of the Gospel of Matthew..

# The Secular Law of Islam

The divine Koran, Torah and Gospel would be the religious law of Islam. All the rest would fall into the category of the secular. But things are not that easy or clear. The hadiths and Shariah have an in-between position according to some people. And, according to others, the religious law of the Scriptures is also to be supplemented by commentary and rulings of the learned.

The king's law, which is used here as a proxy for the law of any form of secular government, starts this section. It is followed by a discussion of the hadiths and Shariah, which some Muslim claim to be law.

## THE KING'S LAW

The propriety of having a body of secular law, or the king's law as it might be called in those days, is recognized in the divine Koran. The Koran effectively authorizes the existence of secular law and also instructs Muslims to obey those laws:

*Joseph had to abide by the Egyptian king's law while in Egypt (12.76).*

*Allah strengthened his [King David's] kingdom and gave him sound judgment and wisdom to help him rule (38.20).*

*Allah commands you to turn over the duties of government to worthy people and, when you judge them, you should judge with justice (4.58).*

*Affairs should be decided by taking counsel amongst yourselves (42.38).*

*Obey Allah and those in authority among you (4.59).*

The Koran contains some rules that could be considered more secular than religious, but inclusion in the Koran gives them religious law status. An example would be the inheritance rules. They are few, numbering under 100.

A more meaningful Koranic contribution to the secular arises from the ethical standards set forth by Allah. Those standards, like that of fairness and justice, provide overall guidance for the writing of secular law. But in terms of specifics governing how the people should lead their day-to-day secular lives, there is very little in the Koran.

## THE KORAN DOES NOT AIM AT COVERING SECULAR LAW

It would be most difficult to maintain that Islam, as presented in the Koran, aims at covering all aspects of Muslim secular life. Allah revealed the Koran and explained all things (16.89) in full detail (6.114), but that relates only to the spiritual welfare of man. That is, the Koran explained all religious things, which is what is expected of a Scripture.

If the Koran was also meant to cover all aspects of secular life, there would be no need for the king's law which the Koran specifically recognizes and authorizes. Also, if the Koran were intended to encompass secular law, there would be precious little secular law (limited to less than 100 as previously referred to) because Allah had given no one authority to add to His revelations (7.33).

# The Hadiths

The hadiths represent the words and deeds of the Prophet Muhammad in the secular world of Arabia of that time. Muhammad was born in 570, started receiving the revelations in 610 and died in 632. It was an agrarian society, and not a very advanced one. The proposition underlying the hadiths is that Muhammad was the model Muslim and thus anything he said and did was to be followed by other Muslims, with some viewing the hadiths as if they were law.

There was no actual record of what Muhammad said and did during the period. Few people were educated, few knew how to write (or read) and writing materials were not as easy to come by and had a short self-life. With little of Muhammad's recitals of Allah's revelations having been contemporaneously recorded, it can be assumed that there was nothing or almost nothing written about Muhammad's day-to-day words and deeds. But the oral tradition was strong in those days and Muhammad's companions and others who were in close proximity to him likely passed on his words and deeds orally.

The hadiths weren't assembled and compiled until some 200 years after the death of the Prophet. That means that the hadiths were orally passed from person to person for about ten generations, not something that adds to reliability.

## RELIABILITY

In the intervening 200 years, the recollections of the oral transmitters could have been subject to a number of pressures. First and foremost must have been the Koran as it finally appeared. Consciously or subconsciously, believers could have embellished their recollections along the lines that would have been suggested by the Koran. Or the devout could have subjectively incorporated the Koranic dictates in recollecting what Muhammad said and did.

Such matters could never be known. Nor could the propensity of people to embellish and wax poetic at campfires, to say nothing of the possibility of storytellers of the day, a foremost entertainment source of ancient times, vying with one another to make their stories more interesting and expand their audiences.

It is no wonder that the compilers of Muhammad's words and deeds were faced with such a horrendous task. First they had to discover, find, and interview those who claimed passed-down oral knowledge. Then they had to determine whether the 200-year backwards trail for each account could possibly be true, and finally they had to evaluate the content, reconcile inconsistencies and choose the final version of Muhammad's words and deeds. It must have been a daunting task. It was said that the compilers had to deal with more than 500,000 discrete recollections.

The compilers were not historians in the sense of being scientists, but were certainly worshippers viewing matters within the context of their personal beliefs. Undoubtedly, the learned (*ulama*) were involved. There was no uniformity of opinion or religious outlook as shown by the inability of the compilers to come up with a single, agreed-to compilation. Each group along the extensive range of opinion wound up writing their own version of the hadiths.

The groups included the "schools of jurisprudence" consisting of *ulama* of like-mind. In time, many of those schools fell by the wayside. Today there are four school of jurisprudence each with its own passed-down compilation of hadiths from the mid-850's or so. They range from very orthodox to very liberal, or, to use different terms, conservative to extreme. While all were undoubtedly devout and pious in their own ways, it would be natural for them to view matters through their own glasses and build-in another type of unreliability atop that arising from having to deal with 200 years of voluminous oral transmissions.

The reliability debate rages because it goes to the very core of the hadiths, and modern scientific inquiry raises still more concerns. But the scientific debate is incomplete, being largely between Muslim theologians and Western scientists. Muslim scientists are yet to voice opinions, apparently not wanting to get involved in his sort of analysis and being content to leave matters of faith where they are. The Western scientists generally find the hadiths to be unreliable, with shade of opinion ranging from rarely giving them any weight to the outspoken condemnation as one of the greatest historical frauds.

Muhammad's own words, appearing in the Koran (6.50, 7.188, 17.93, 46.9), show him to be a mortal messenger, not a lawmaker nor divine. As was previously shown, the Koranic references to wisdom and the Book of Wisdom do not presage the hadiths, but rather are references to the Koran itself (10.1, 31.2-4). Allah views Muhammad as an excellent exemplar (33.21) but still only as a messenger and teacher:

*Allah sent you a messenger from amongst you to recite His revelations and teach you Scripture and wisdom (2.151).*


## HADITHS INCLUDE THE SOCIAL CUSTOMS OF THE TIME (*Sunna*)

In addition to the words and deeds of Muhammad, the hadiths incorporate what is known as the Traditions (*sunna*) or the way the society of his day handled things.  This brings the societal norms of that agrarian society directly into the hadiths.

As a result, the hadiths wind up including what Muhammad said and did, and also included what he didn't say and didn't do (in terms of negative inference).  Things done in Muhammad's presence with his express approval, apparent approval, or without his disapproval were included as hadiths.  If Muhammad did something in a certain way, it became a law specifying that was the way it must be done.  If Muhammad criticized something, it became outlawed.  If Muhammad applauded or failed to criticize something, it became required.

Even where Muhammad was not involved, the custom of the day became law on the basis that Allah would not allow the whole community to establish a custom that was not right.  Yet, this approach carried to its logical extreme would have approved the societal norm of Sodom and Gomorrah where every man in town participated in the wrongdoing.  That is hardly likely, but it does highlight a danger in this approach.

Muslims recognize and honor the hadiths to various degrees, with many viewing the hadiths as being a key component of Islam, or its historic tradition, or as law.

## NOT INCLUDING THE HADITHS IN THE AUHTOR'S STUDY OF THE KORAN

I thought long and hard about the role the hadiths should play in my study of the Koran and concluded that I had no alternative but to omit them. This, after all is a study of the Koran. The hadiths are external to the Koran and, although it is the most important external writing, it is still just one of many external writing. All the external writings are man-made. None are divine like the Koran. They do not belong in a study of the divine.

I have no opinion on the reliability of the hadiths but note that the Koran itself says that no external matter should be used to elaborate or amplify the Koran. The Koran says it explains all things in sufficient detail (3.138, 6.114, 16.89, 17.12) and Allah's revelations should not be supplemented (7.33).

There would be still more reason for not using the hadiths for elaboration or amplification if it is true, as some claim, that the hadiths are so wide-ranging that they can support or contradict most anything.

But I put all this aside and take the simple view that the divine must control over the man-made. Thus, if the hadiths or any other external source contradicts, or can't be supported or found in the Koran, they must yield to the Koran. If they accord with the Koran, they are superfluous.

Either way, the external sources become irrelevant to a study of the divine Koran.

# The Shariah

The Shariah is a combination of the hadiths and those verses from the Koran that relate to secular matters. That is, the 100 or so verses from over 6,000 verses in the Koran that can be said to relate to secular matters were added to the huge amount of material that the schools of jurisprudence took from the hadiths to include in their versions of the Shariah, which they called "holy" law.

If the word "holy" is viewed as referring only to the divine, the Shariah could not be considered "holy" since so little comes from the only divine source Islam has, the Koran. But viewed more expansively and loosely, the Shariah could be viewed as "holy" since it contains some Koranic material. Nevertheless, attaching the word "holy" to what is clearly secular law would seem to transform the secular into the religious, a characterization that doesn't seem to fit the facts.

Shariah law is very time and place specific. It captures and freezes the way of life of an Arabian community, a desert agrarian community, and would apply the secular laws governing such a society to a modern society. With the Shariah being based on the 7$^{th}$ century hadiths, or perhaps it was of the 9$^{th}$ century as that was when the hadiths were compiled and the customs and practices of that age might have crept into the compilation, the time disconnect becomes obvious. But it is not accidental or incidental for the proponents of Shariah can be said to prefer the old ways.

Neither does Shariah portray what the secular laws would have looked like in a non-Arabic community, nor in a big city like Damascus, or anywhere else. The 7$^{th}$ to 9$^{th}$ century Arabian Peninsula is thus advanced as the secular legal model for the entire Muslim world today -- for the 21$^{st}$ century and for places as far flung as Indonesia, places with a totally different climates, heritages, cultures and community practices.

Time and place change things significantly, and the Shariah has to be modified, revised, or adjusted to apply it of the new time and place. Under the Shariah approach, what exists today must be projected back in time to see how that matter would have been handled in the ancient days, and that would substitute for an independent secular determination as to how the matter should be handled today under current conditions.

Naturally, members of the current day *ulama* would control making these modifications, but first they would have to get the modern Muslim nation to adopt Shariah law. It is not like religious law of the Koran which automatically applies in all Muslim nations. The Shariah has to be adopted by the secular government for it to become the secular law of the land.

The adoption of the Shariah as the law of the land would disenfranchise the existing legislative body, be that a parliament or monarchy, and effectively substitute the *ulama* of one of the schools of jurisprudence for the secular legislative body, law interpreter and law enforcer. This explains why strong secular rulers from the Mongols to the Ottoman, and a modern ruler like Ataturk (in Turkey) would not have the Shariah as the law of their lands.

Thus, adoption of Shariah Law is most controversial and promises to be hard fought in a modern Muslim nation. The opponents of Shariah could be expected to argue that the hadiths are not authorized by the Koran, that they contradict the Koran, are inappropriate for a modern society, and that their reliability is not certain.

The proponents of the Shariah will argue that the religious and secular spheres should be one as they were in the days of Muhammad and that tradition requires the adoption of Shariah. They would also argue that the ancient way of life was better. Within the *ulama*, each school of jurisprudence will continue to argue for their own version of Shariah as there is no religious hierarchy in Islam to force them to coalesce.

# Absence of a Religious Hierarchy

Islam does not have an authorized religious hierarchy because the Koran does not provide for one. The Koran does not recognize any religious office, institution or role for anybody or any group. As a result, each Muslim can have a very close and very personal individual relationship with Allah without any clergy or other intermediary. And Allah does not require that believers be extremely pious or monastic:

*Pious monastic life is the innovation of others, not Allah. Allah requires only that believers please Him by right observance (57.27).*

On the same token, the absence of a religious hierarchy also means that there is no authorized institutionalized religious body in Islam to make rules, draw lines, or reconcile differences. There is no hierarchy to approve or disapprove religious rulings, and by so doing allow a coherent religious law to evolve.

Without there being any religious body able to cull the morass of religious commentary, rulings and precedents handed down from generation to generation over the centuries, the accumulations just continue to pile up. The sheer volume would seem to allow a significant degree of picking and choosing to support positions.

The matter of religious authority has been ripping-up

Islam since the days of the Caliphate. Initially the caliph, the secular leader, was given authority over the religion with the requirement that the people be consulted on significant matters. The people had a direct relationship with Allah and that effectively gave them the right to vote. Muslims who knew the recitals of Muhammad were entitled to have an opinion and vote on the religious issues referred to them by the caliph.

That dissipated in time as the learned ones, the *ulama*, developed and grew powerful, first aggregating to themselves the vote on the religious issues referred by the secular leader and then creating a clergy to interpose themselves in the relationship to Allah. Ordinary Muslims were cut-out, pushed back. But still, there was no authorized religious leader. Religious law was determined by each group of *ulama* or even by an individual learned person with the right to issue *fatwa* being innovated in time.

While it seems that the *ulama* had the means to convince ordinary Muslims to accept their religious authority, they didn't seem able to induce other *ulama* to accepting their authority. Thus, Islamic religious society became factionalized, contrary to the wishes of Allah who forbids sects:

*Keep your bond to Allah and be all together, not disunited (3.103).*
*Do not disagree and become divided in religion (3.105).*
*Do not split up the religion by breaking into sects (6.159).*

As there is no authorized religious hierarchy, the various groups of *ulama* can't be forced to yield to one another or arrive at a consensus. Each group apparently feels itself free to go its own way even though that disobeys the Koranic command to be all together.

This is important to the extremists amongst the *ulama*, as they could not have long survived had the Koran authorized a religious hierarchy that could review what they said and did in the name of Islam. As it is, nobody has the authority to declare the extremists or any other group or sect to be wrong or out of line, except other Muslims acting in accordance with Koranic directives. And the use of religious rulings, also unauthorized in the Koran, appears to compound matters.

# Rulings, Commentary & Codification

Rulings (*fatwa*) are given precedential value by some Muslims, effectively treating the rulings as one would treat formal judicial decision. That greatly expands the body of Islamic law, whether the precedent is considered binding or merely influential. As these ruling carry down to the present through the centuries, the body of such Islamic law expands exponentially. And, in the nature of things, the rulings would range over the entire gamut of views and could serve as support for many legal positions. The ability to pick and choose does not yield much legal certainty.

The commentaries of scholars, teachers and theologians are usually influential in any society. The texts, handed-down over the centuries, also cover the full gamut of opinion. Although these texts generally make no claim as to being law, they are accorded as much honor and precedential value as a person chooses to grant them. There could be support for virtually everything.

The combination of centuries of rulings and commentary makes for an unwieldy and unclear body of "law" and creates an unrestrained legal environment. Shades of that have been seen in *fatwa* wars. One learned person writes a *fatwa* attacking another's religious position, or attacking another person personally, and the other responds in-kind, and so on.

The *fatwa* rulings process was originally designed to answer the religious questions of faithful Muslims, akin to the *responsa* of the rabbis in Judaism from which the *fatwa* probably evolved. But the use of *fatwa* expanded in a potentially lethal way as a *fatwa* could demand death; that is, the *fatwa* could becomes an order to execute a person, bypassing normal judicial proceedings.

That was seen when the Ayatollah Khomeini issued a

*fatwa* condemning the famous Muslim author Salman Rushdie to death for apostasy because of a novel Rushdie wrote. Rushdie took it seriously and hid and traveled with bodyguards until the *fatwa* was lifted.

Some *fatwa* carry more weight than other *fatwa* and are more influential based on the reputation of the person issuing the ruling. The *fatwa* continue to stand for what they contain since there is no one to correct or cull them in order to establish a cohesive body of law. Later generations are free to rely on whatever they like, or ignore them all. They have pilled-up over the centuries and the entire morass comes down to the current day.

An alternative is to codify Islamic law, as the Ottoman did in the Majalla Code. An analogy might be drawn to the Emperor Napoleon codifying existing French law into the coherent Napoleonic Code, making whatever judgments, selections and modifications necessary to do so. So did the Ottoman, who then ruled the Islamic world.

The Ottoman felt that their legal structure gave jurists carte blanch to decide anything in any way they wished, and felt it gave extremists too much leeway to interfere with Ottoman control and domination of Islam. They might have also felt that the codification process allowed compromise and consensus along the lines specified in the Koran (42.38). However, that was not to be as codification in Islam could not withstand *ulama* opposition.

Chapter Four

# Separation of Mosque & State
# and
# Islam's Democratic Leanings

Almost from its very beginning, Islam had a problem as to the separation of the religious and secular spheres, or, as called here, the separation of Mosque and state. The Prophet Muhammad had combined religious and secular authority over his society and was extraordinarily successful at it. His personal statature and outstanding results in combining mosque and state raised an issue for future generations of Muslims as to whether that set a required pattern for Islam.

Neither Muhammad nor the revelations of Allah provided any direct guidance for the succession of either religious or secular leadership. Allah was silent as to religious leadership. Allah did not speak of religious leadership or hierarchy, except to say that Muhammad was the last of the prophets (33.40). This might be viewed as suggesting the bond of mosque and state was to be broken after Muhammad, but Muslims do not take it that way. The Koran frequently mentions monarchies, where succession is frequently father to son, and also mentions that Muslims should choose their leaders (4.58-59, 42.38), basically leaving secular leadership and the form of government up to the secular society to decide.

Muhammad was also silent as to succession, perhaps because he had no living son. But yet the Koran speaks of truth and justice even though it be against family (4.135, 6.152), so it is not at all clear that Muhammad would have favored family. These verses point to other things possibly being more important than family ties, so perhaps the father should not automatically favor the son. Muhammad surely had the opportunity to speak out on succession and obviously chose not to do so.

As a result, there is no guidance in Islam from either Allah or Muhammad as to succession in either the religious or secular spheres. However, there is a possible exception arising from Allah not having authorized a religious hierarchy and announcing that Muhammad was the last of the prophets in that it might be said to implicitly reject the concept of religious leadership. That would leave only secular leadership and all Muslims having a direct relationship with Allah without there being a religious leader or religious intermediation.

Thus, the method of identification, legitimacy and authority of all future rulers was left in doubt, as was the nature of future rule.  As it turned out, Muhammad's successor was said to be selected by acclamation of the entire Muslim community or, more probably in my view, the selection was by made by an elite group consisting of Muhammad's close compatriots and military aids with a consensus of sorts amongst those necessarily being involved.  Either way, shades of democracy lurk as the selection of the first caliph was obviously based on the merits, the best man for the job at the time.

That man, Abu Bakr, was not the most talented leader or general but was the best man to keep Islam together as many tribes wanted to leave the army on the death of Muhammad.  The first caliph was a distinct success in this, effectively saving Islam.  The apparent arrangement that was worked out was that Abu Bakr had secular control and had to get the concurrence of the community on important religious decisions.  This left the religious authority with the community of ordinary Muslims, which was later seized by the learned *ulama* amongst them.

In time, the Caliphate was undermined by those of the *ulama* who had the mind, will and ability to do so.  When a caliph commanded the religious, his authority was questioned.  When a caliph separated himself from religion or kept his distance, his piety was questioned.  Those *ulama* spoke out and kept the pot stirred.

Those *ulama* evolved into more recognizable forms by the 9th century with their four separate schools of religious jurisprudence. There were unconnected schools because those *ulama* couldn't agree amongst themselves on how to "interpret" the Koran since each group had its own agenda and views, a pattern that continues to today. Underlying the division was the absence of any a clear designation of religious authority from the Koran, as no one had the authority to force a consensus.

The battle between those in the *ulama* and the Caliphate came to a head in the 9th century when the ruling Abbasids, having been in power for almost a century, considered the idea of codifying Islamic law. The codification would wrest the legal system from the hands of the *ulama* and leave the *ulama* with a much curtailed role.

The Abbasids were collateral relatives of Muhammad and thus Arab, but they were close to the Persians and their power base was in the Shiite areas north of Arabia. In contrast to the Sunni in Arabia, the Shiite believed in an Imamate with the Imam having both supreme religious and secular authority, effectively sanctioning the combination of Mosque and state. Centuries later, the Ayatollah Khomeini claimed to represent the hidden Imam when he took over in Iran, setting the Iranian pattern of combining Mosque and state -- control over the secular is maintained by the religious authority choosing who may run for secular office.

The Abbasids conducted an inquisition (*mihna*) requiring, amongst other things, that the *ulama* publicly concede that their role in religion was subservient to the Caliphate, but that effort was abandoned. The *ulama* won the battle, becoming the clear religious leaders. The stage was now reversed with the *ulama* trying to seize secular control so that they would have both religious and secular control.

And so it went, with the pendulum swinging back and forth in an endless battle for power. Today, some Muslim countries are under the control of some group of *ulama* and other Muslim countries are the control of a secular government.

The countries that have adopted Shariah law fall in the *ulama* camp and usually combine Mosque and state in some way. Where secular authorities control the national government, there is separation of Mosque and state. Thus, it cannot be said that Islam either favors or shuns separation of religion and state.

The Turkish example provides some interesting history. Turkey had developed a strong secular sphere and clearly separated religion from state. It is no wonder that Osama bin Laden had identified the creation of the secular Muslim state in Turkey some 80 years before he spoke out as the very thing which would eventually, in his view, undermine the Islamic state. As bin-Laden saw it, both spheres should be under the control of the religious leader, like in a Taliban state. Turkey had obliterated *ulama* power, even taking away their charitable endowments. Curtailing the critical role charitable funding played in the support of the *ulama* had been a key element of Ataturk's secularization program. Many Islamic counties today have secular governments and have separated Mosque and state to varying extents.

But what does the Koran say?

## THE KORAN RECOGNIZES THE EXISTENCE OF SEPARATE STATES WITH THEIR OWN LAWS AND THE SEPARATION OF MOSQUE AND STATE

The Koran recognizes the existence of separate states, referring both to the king's law in Egypt and the king's law in King David's Kingdom of Israel. The king's law is obviously being distinguished from Allah's religious law:

*Joseph had to abide by the Egyptian king's law while in Egypt (12.76).*

*Allah made you [King David] a ruler on earth, so judge justly and do not follow personal desires (38.26).*

*Allah strengthened his [King David's] kingdom and gave him sound judgment and wisdom to help him rule (38.20).*

Allah allows a nation to have its own secular laws, and

forbids them to be in Allah's name:

*Do not associate with Allah that for which He has given you no authority in His revelations (7.33).*

Also, as we have seen, the Koran also instructs man to create secular governance, and then obey those who govern. The requirement that decisions should be reached by taking counsel of one another seems to bespeak of democracy or presage democracy:

*Allah commands you to turn over the duties of government to worthy people (4.58).*
*Obey Allah and those in authority among you (4.59).*
*Affairs should be decided by taking counsel amongst yourselves (42.38).*

The Koran's acceptance of the Gospel (3.3) also supports the separation of religion and state. The Christian Gospel of Matthew states: "Render therefore to Caesar the things which are Caesar's; and unto God the things that are God's (Matthew 22:21)." That is considered to be the foundation for the separation of church and state in Christianity.

The Jewish experience is equally telling for Islam. Like the Gospel, Allah accepts the Torah (3.3). Moses and later King David were the clear secular leaders while the separate priesthood had a chief priest, the first being Aaron, and their own line of succession. Thus there was clear separation of Temple and state in Judaism as well as Christianity. Since there is nothing in the Koran to abrogate this, the precedent flowing from the prior Scriptures should have weight in Islam.

The Romans tore down the Jerusalem Temple in the year 70 AC, some 6 centuries before Allah revealed the Koran. With the destruction of the Temple, the scripturally authorized Jewish priesthood disappeared. The rabbinate of the synagogues ursurped religious authority, having no support or authority from the Jewish Scripture. When Allah revealed the Koran in the 7th century, He made no mention of a religious clergy or hierarchy for Islam.

## FORMS OF SECULAR GOVERNMENT

While the Koran recognized and authorizes the existence of a separate secular government, it does not specifically address the form of such government. The Koran gives legitimacy to the monarchy as an acceptable form of government because it is mentioned any number of times, monarchies being the common form of government in ancient times, not because the Koran recognizes any divine right of kings.

But the form could be anything: a monarchy, a republic, a limited constitutional parliament, a limited monarchy, a constitutional legislature under a monarchy, a democracy or even a dictatorship. However, it would seem that the Koranic reference to the people forming the government (4.58) and consultation and consensus amongst the people (42.38), would require that the secular government be representative government or include a representative parliament representing the community of Muslims.

But the people could instead select a king. The selection of the first caliph was essentially the selection of a king, but as was shown in the selection of the second caliph, the Caliphate did not include the right to select a successor. What the events after the death of Muhammad do show was that the power was in the people, perhaps in their elite, but still in the people with no automatic right of succession. The Caliphate did not pass from father to son.

## THE KORAN'S CONCEPT OF UNITY

The Koran constantly refers to unity but it should not be taken as a directive that the whole world be one nation. The Koran mentions the existence of nations, towns, townships, tribes, families and peoples, sometimes almost interchangeably, all in the sense of their being distinct secular units or communities.

Mankind is said to be one community, one nation, one humanity, created from the same being and living on the same earth under the same canopy. Nowhere is there any Koranic suggestion that the various nations or peoples be merged or combined in any sense so as to become a single state. To the contrary, the Koran contemplates and directs that they remain separate:

*All of mankind is a single community (2.213).*

*Mankind was created from a single pair, male and a female, and made into tribes and nations so that they might know one another (49.13).*

*Allah could have chosen to make all the peoples a single people, but made them as they are in order to try them as they vie with one another in good works (5.48).*

As the Koran expressed it, Allah does not require and does not want nations to merge and become one. But He wants unity in faith. That is, the faith should be one and the same for all Muslims. As the existence of sects conflicts with the requirement of unity, the Koran specifically forbids the establishments of sects:

*Keep your bond to Allah and be all together, not disunited (3.103).*

*All believers are brethren and you have a duty to make peace between your contending brethren (49.10).*

*If parties of believers quarrel, make peace between them with fairness and justice (49.9).*

*Do not split up the religion by breaking into sects (6.159).*

Since the Koran is referring to a brotherhood in faith, the mutual accountability and personal and financial responsibility found between blood brothers does not necessarily apply. Muslims are not accountable to one another, and, as a corollary, they are not responsible for one another.  They are brothers in sharing a common faith, but no more:

> *Those who turn into believers, pray regularly and give charity become your brothers in faith (9.11).*
>
> *Although you are not accountable to other believers for anything and they are not accountable to you for anything, do not drive other believers away from Allah (6.52).*

Yet, the claim is heard that there is one Islam, that the religion and the state are one and that all nations are one. There is unity in faith in the Koran, but that is all there is concerning unity.  All else is negated by the Koran  -- states remain separate, the religion and state are separate, and the brotherhood is not a blood brotherhood of accountability and responsibility.

Yet, it is the expanded "unity" that has become the cry of the extremist *ulama*.  This cry underpins the extremist *ulama* ambitious goal for the widespread adoption of Shariah, their weapon of choice in their battle to obtain control over the secular governments and thus achieve the oneness they seek, under themselves.

Rather, it would seem that the Koran stands against the combining of Mosque and state based on a relatively good case that can be made from the Koran itself.  But that can't be advanced with any degree of certainty because the Koran does not say so in plain words.  It is a reasonable interpretation, but as I said numerous times, the Koran itself negates any interpretations of its plain words, relying only in what flows naturally from those words.

So it would not seem right to say that the Koran bars the combination of Mosque and state. But on the same token, it would not seem right to say that the Koran requires the combination of Mosque and state. What does seem clear, however, is that it is up to the community of Muslims to decide.

Chapter Five

# Fundamentalism, Extremism & Terrorism

Fundamentalism is one of those "hot" words that have many meanings. Discussing what fundamentalism is, might be, or should be, will not solve any problems nor resolved any issues. Nor will it convince anyone that they are wrong side of Allah, as everyone will remain convinced that they are on the right side. However, delving into the meaning of fundamentalism, and its reputed handmaidens of extremism and terrorism, could help clarify what the issues are and what is at stake.

## FINDING A WORKABLE DEFINITION OF FUNDAMENTALISM

All believers believe in the fundamentals of their religions, viewing the fundamentals through their own glasses. When their views are consistent with the plain words of the Scripture, believers are in agreement with one another and the fundamentals of that religion are being adhered to. However, if "interpretations" of the Scripture creep in, differences between believers necessarily arise and make the fundamentals difficult to identify and practices vary.

Once believers depart from the pain words of the Scripture, their "interpretations" can and do vary wildly. Where those interpretations are logical and reasonable, it might be tempting to accept them as falling within the contemplation of the Scripture. However, the Koran makes it difficult to adopt this view for Islam.

The Koran does not leave any room for interpretations. As we have seen, and this is worth repeating, the Koran abounds with strictures against Muslims making their own interpretations since the Koran already explains all things and in plain language:

*The Koran was sent to you explained in full detail (6.114).*
*Allah has revealed the Koran to you explaining all things (16.89).*
*Allah has expounded on everything with distinctive explanation (17.12).*
*Do not associate with Allah that for which He has given you no authority in His revelations, nor say about Allah that which you cannot know (7.33).*
*Do not alter words from their context nor neglect a portion of what the Koran says (5.13).*
*The Koran is a Book of wisdom made plain (11.1).*
*The Koran consists of two types of verses. There are the*

*basic verses of substance that have clear and established meaning. The others are allegorical verses the meanings of which are known only to Allah and cannot be known by man, and yet man causes discord by seeking to explain them (3.7).*

Thus, the Koran is saying that the basic, fundamental verses of the Koran require no interpretation and that interpretation of the allegorical verses is also inappropriate but for a different reason. Man does not know and cannot know the meaning of the allegorical verses and should not be interpreting them.

The net result is that none of the verses of the Koran should be subject to interpretation. Curiously, the Koran notes that man nevertheless offers interpretations of the allegorical, but is silent about the other verses. Perhaps it was that those verses were so clear, so fully explained in detail, that there was just no basis for interpretation and men wouldn't try. But they do.

Simply put, if you believe in and follow the plain meaning of a Scripture, you believe in the fundamentals of the religion and you are a fundamentalist in the fullest sense of that word. If you feel it necessary to add, subtract or modify the plain words of the Scripture, you are innovating and departing in one way or another from what the Scripture fundamentally says.

Any label given to that, from conservative to liberal,

from freeing to restrictive, would be self-serving and pejorative since the labeling is necessarily based on personal views.  There is no label to be accorded to those who follow the plain meaning of the Koran except that they are true believers and that they are in fundamental agreement with one another.

What seems to complicate matters in Islam is that the honor so rightly conferred on Muhammad and his times is elevated by some in the *ulama* to such sacred status that his words and deeds (hadiths) are sometimes used to interpret the Koran.  Yet the Koran clearly pointed out that Muhammad himself said that he not divine and not an angel, but rather was a mere mortal messenger.  However, it seems that those in the *ulama* who have their own agenda elevate the words and deeds of Muhammad rather than stick to the plain meaning of the Koran.

My view is that "fundamentalism" contemplates adhering the plain meaning of one's own Scripture and would be in conflict with any label such as orthodox, conservative, strict or liberal.  In the West, the word "fundamentalism" seems to have had its first application to Protestants in the United States who were litigating in the civil courts a matter they thought offensive to their religion. The name stuck, but it had no real meaning other that the fundamentalist believes in his or her Scripture.

## THE NEED FOR FUNDAMENTALISM

In many societies, including those in the West, there is a need for spirituality and faith and the personal security and happiness that provides. Standards have become particularly important as religion and religious beliefs are being pulled in many directions by believers. The need for fundamentalism is a need for standards; religious standards founded in the fundamentals of the religion. The converse of religious fundamentalism would be a form of looseness under a society without standards or with minimal standards.

An analogy might be made to the world of art, where Marcel Duchamp (1887-1968) convinced others that *Art was what he said it was* because he was an artist and able to make such a determination. Duchamp had merely placed his signature on a urinal and deemed it to be a work of art, demanding that the art world accept it as such.

In a way, Duchamp's edict became a very freeing moment for the art world because anything became acceptable in art. Anybody could do anything and say it was art. But along with this freedom, came the elimination of all artistic standards, elimination of all concerns for aesthetics, beauty or anything else. The words "aesthetics" and "beauty" became banal, of no account and not to be spoken of. Excrement soon became an artistic material. Duchamp's edict became objectionable to many in the art world.

The religious equivalent would be some religious leader saying that *Religion is what he says it is*. That cannot be acceptable. Some grounding principles are required. The grounding principles are provided by the fundamentals of a religion, which can only be found in its divine Scripture. That, in turn, requires reliance on a fair reading of the plain words of the Scripture. Anything else would lead to a person with religious frock issuing edicts as to what the religion is. It may be okay for Duchamp to assume the role of a god in art, but it clearly isn't okay in religion. Fundamentalism, standards, emanate only from the plain words of the Scripture.

## KORANIC FUNDAMENTALISM

Devotion to Allah in Islam is extremely broad reaching, extensive and intensive. The five "pillars" of Islam are the five obligatory requirements for Muslims:
1. Belief in the divine unity, that is, belief in the one and only God.
2. The ritual prayers (*salat*), done daily.
3. Fasting during the month of Ramadan.
4. The payment of the tax (*zakat*) to help the poor.
5. The once a lifetime pilgrimage (hajj) to Mecca for those who can afford it.

The word "pillar" is not to be found in the Koran. It is a man-made construction based on these requirements being laid out plainly and emphasized throughout the Koran.

Islam is said to be unique in that it requires total submission, but all religions require submission, compliance, or allegiance with the degree of submission not really measurable. The name "Islam" itself means submission, essentially the surrender to God.

The surrender itself, consecrated only by a recital of words, makes that person a Muslim without any formal ritual or baptismal. It is a profession of faith uttered aloud, and called the *Shahadah*: "There is no god other than Allah and Muhammad is his messenger." With this oral expression of faith in Allah, a person is recognized as being a Muslim.

Praying is not a matter of going to a house of worship once a week or on special holiday occasions, as sometimes prevails in the West, but prayer is woven into everyday life in Islam. Muslims pray three to five times a day, facing Mecca since the direction was changed from facing Jerusalem early in Islam's history. Mosques are places for worship although prayers might be offered anywhere. The prayer requirements serve to keep Islam in the forefront of daily Muslim thought and make for unity in faith. However, Allah does not require Muslims to become pious like monks in a monastery (57.27).

Ramadan, the month of fasting, has a similar binding effect. It should be understood that Muslims do not go on a total fast for a month, but rather fast during the day and are free to eat at night.

The payment of the poor tax, a pillar of Islam, is part of a much more extensive charitable tradition in Islam. Traditional giving to charity regularly, including hand-outs to beggars, goes much further than paying the poor tax.

The *hajj* is not like a sightseeing trip to Rome, but is an extensive, fully planned ritual where a white garment must be worn and guides engaged. Chanting is pervasive, rites are performed for days, and long circuit walks are required with assistance being provided to those who need it. Up to a million people a day share the quest when the heat can approach 120 degrees. The *hajj* has to be one of mankind's remarkable experiences.

The *hajj* necessitated the construction of extensive facilities and airports just used for a couple of months every year. The *hajj* provides fees and earnings for many Muslims and confers much honor and influence within Islam on those who administer it. Historically, the control of Mecca has led to many wars over the centuries. The hajj is an exceptional rite available only to Muslims, extending the religious bond and further binding Muslim to Muslim.

But a fair reading of the Koran shows that Allah requires more than the five pillars. Allah requires that He be obeyed and that His way, path or cause be followed. He requires Muslims to adhere to ethical principles of justice, fairness, compassion and mercy, all to be found in the Koran and fundamental to Islam. Thus, the fundamentals of Islam rest on its pillars, its ethical principles and its direct commands and limitations.

There is still more. Allah expects Muslims to do good deeds and those deed play an important role on judgment day. There are no absolutions in Islam. Nothing is forgiven or forgotten. Everything will be before Allah on the day of judgment and the doing of good deeds will help to favorably balance the scale. This is a lifetime endeavor as lifetime records are kept. And there is nothing to indicate whether a quantitative or qualitative balance will be struck. Thus, doing good deeds play an extremely important role in Islam even though it isn't listed as part of the pillars as such:

*There are those who know all that you do and write it down (82.10-12).*

*Every man's actions will cling to his neck and Allah will bring his book of account wide open for him to see on the day of judgment (17.13-14).*

*Allah will justly balance a person's good and evil deeds so as not to wrong anyone in the slightest degree on the day of judgment (21.47).*

## THE OPPOSITE OF FUNDAMENTALISM IS NOT SECULARISM

The extremist *ulama* oppose the modern "secular" society, viewing it to be contrary to the dictates of Islam as they see it. They effectively view the ancient way of life in the days of Muhammad as being fundamental to the religion, while the Koran says nothing of the kind.

The Koran recognizes the separateness of secular life under the king's law, law that changes in time and place. Joseph was acknowledged to live under the king's law of Egypt, and King David made his own law (12.76, 38.20). The Koranic instructions to make over the trusts of government and obey the selected leaders (4.58-59) have no time or place limitations nor does the requirement that affairs should be decided by consultation and consensus (42.38) within the community. These are all references to a secular society, to the contemporaneous secular society.

The Koran is eternal and the fundamentals of the religion will remain as such throughout time, while the secular society is acknowledged to change in time. The everlasting fundamentals of the religion and the changing secular society are not in opposition to each other but go together, each in its own way. The extremist *ulama* attempt to reign in the changing secular society by lashing it to the ancient society as if the fundamentals of the religion required it. It doesn't.

Having said this, I realize that many people believing in many religions have fond spots in their hearts for the "old days" and the "old religion." While one can hark back to the "old days," there is really no "old religion" as the religions and their scriptural cores do not change. Social customs change.

The Koran remained exactly the same all the time, and the plain meaning of its words hasn't changed. People just lived differently in the old days and that underpinned the longing for the past. The fundamentals of the religions are still the same as they have always been. Perhaps religious rituals, those not based on Scripture, changed but not the fundamentals of the religion.

It should be noted that harking back to an ancient time still leaves you in a secular society; the secular society of that day. Muhammad's society was a secular society, a secular society of that day and age with its own customs and ways of doing things. Recall, the *sunna* of Muhammad's day was added to the hadiths.

Thus, every age has its own secular society and it is just that those who hark back to ancient times prefer one secular society to another. Yet, they use the "secular" label pejoratively, as if there is something wrong with it and as if they weren't harkening back to a secular society. The simple explanation is that those who hark back to a previous time merely prefer that time. For the *ulama* who hark back, that time happens to be when the secular society was dominated by religious interests, like in the Taliban society.

People live in an ever changing secular world unless they are in a monastery, which Allah would shun. Yet they are labeled "secularists," as if it or the word "secular" denotes people who do not believe in religion. These terms are used pejoratively by the extremist *ulama*, aimed at intimidating those they would dominate.

It's just a step away from calling a Muslim a non-Muslim or even a barbarian, which are insults hurled by the extremists at those they would cower. This had been a tool of extremist for centuries while the Koran accepts all who believe and utter the required profession of faith. Islam doesn't discriminate against novices:

*Those who submit to Islam should be accepted as Muslims even if faith hasn't yet entered their hearts (49.14).*

Islamic secular society and Islam's fundamental beliefs are not in opposition to one another. Only the extremists are in opposition to a secular society governed by secularists.

## EXTREMISM & TERRORISM

Within this context of "fundamentalism," an extremist

would be a person who departs from the plain meaning of the Scripture in an extreme or radical fashion. A person can have extreme views without being a terrorist. The extremists are those who do not adopt heinous methods to impose their views or inflict harm on others. The terrorist inflicts harm as they attempt to impose their views on others. However you view these terms, definitions yield no real insight nor solve anything. Specific illustrations would be more meaningful.

Take music. The Koran says nothing about music and yet in the history of Islam there were those of the *ulama* who opposed music as being in contravention of Islam, and they actually killed people for it. The Koran and the prior Scriptures have many references to trumpets, but that instrument can be viewed as a communication device to gather people or alert them. However, the prior Scriptures have many references to music and song with nothing being derogatory, which should have some relevance in Islam as Allah also revealed those Scriptures.

Nevertheless, opposing music was a clear innovation on the Koran and can be called extremist or radical. It can also be viewed as disobeying and dishonoring the Koran which would attract penalties:

*Do not associate with Allah that for which He has given you no authority in His revelations (7.33).*
*You should not forbid the good things which Allah has made lawful for believers (5.87).*
*Muslims who disobey Allah should fear the retribution of*

*a grievous day (6.15).*

Maintaining an anti-music position shouldn't be objectionable to others as long as the extremist maintains the position only for oneself. If that person would not play or listen to music, or would leave a place where music is being played, I cannot imagine anyone objecting. But when that person attempts to impose the position on others, as by turning off music played by others or killing those who make music, it becomes objectionable and against the way of Allah. If killing is involved, it becomes terrorist in nature. It is the attempted imposition of one's positions on others that crosses the line.

Another type of an extremist position is one that misrepresents what is actually contained in the Koran. Take the case of the so-called "verse of the sword" which the firebrand *ulama* quote out of context as the Koranic justification for jihads against disbelievers (pagans, idolaters, polytheists, infidels). The firebrands neglect to mention that the pagans attacked the Muslims first, which follows in just a few verses and addresses the same incident:

**Fight and kill pagans wheresoever you find them, seize them as captives, beleaguer them, and lie in wait to ambush them (9.5).**

**Fight those pagans who violated their oaths, assailed your religion and attacked you first (9.13).**

Strangely enough, the firebrand rhetoric is used by the

extremist *ulama* to further their evil cause and the same rhetoric is also used by those who bash Islam and call it evil. Both disregard the plain words of the Koran, this time by omitting a portion of what the Koran says, and do so deliberately in pursuit of their own agendas. They effectively support each other, right in the face of Koran denying both of them and commanding an extra penalty:

*Do not alter words from their context nor neglect a portion of what the Koran says (5.13).*

*Whoever helps a good cause will have its reward and whoever helps an evil cause will bear the burdens of it (4.85).*

*Everyone will bear their own evil burdens in full on the day of judgment, and also the evil burdens of any unkowledgeable people they misled (16.25).*

There is much more that can be said about such omissions and other ways of misrepresenting the Koran. Extensive explanations are included in the Appendix under *"Responding to the Ayatollah Khomeini, Osama Bin-Laden & Hizbullah."*

It would seem that the world could live with extremists of any persuasion as long as they don't try to impose their view on others through violent means -- those are the terrorists. The difficulty, thus, seems to arise from those who insist that their views are the correct views and the only correct views, and then try to impose those views on others through the use of force.

## EXTREMISM IN ISLAMIC HISTORY

Extremism in Islam appears to date back to the Kharijite in Arabia and in what is now called Iraq, Iran and Afghanistan. They came on the scene some 10 years after Muhammad's death and were a force by the time of the fourth caliph, Ali, who they killed in 660. That was less than 10 years after the final compilation of the Koran. That act, the killing of Ali, appears to be the first terrorist act in Islam.

The Kharijite felt that they represented the pure religion, that they had the right to declare other Muslims traitors to the religion, the right to label other Muslims (including Ali) as non-Muslims and kill them, and the right to use unjust jihads to expand the religion. It is said that they created the House of Peace (Islam) versus the House of War (everywhere else) dichotomy that is so hateful outside Islam. The Kharijite had a military wing and fought battles. That was to become the future pattern of extremism; self-directed piousness imposed on others.

The four schools of jurisprudence followed. Muhammad ibn al-Shafi (d820) was the founder of a very extremist school that considered killing non-believers to be a justifiable jihad even if the non-believers did nothing aggressive; clearly against the dictates of the Koran which, by that time, was widely distributed and in hand. This too set a pattern; the Koran would be disregarded with hoped for impunity by those who chose to do so.

Other schools of jurisprudence were the Hanifa (named for Abu Hanifa d767), the Maliki (Malik ibn Anas d795), and the Hanbali (Ahmad ibn Halbal d855). These founders set the theology with the actual schools of jurisprudence being formed by their students and disciples after their deaths. The Shafi may have once been the dominant Sunni in Arabia, and they and the Hanbali were primarily associated with the compilation of the hadiths.

At that time, there were some Muslims, then call "scripturalists," who just relied on the Koran and rejected the hadiths as a source of religious law. Others wanted more religious law to choose from and the hadiths spring up as that source of law, effectively converting the secular law of the ancient days of Muhammad into the so-called religious law of the Shariah. The Shariah, as such, has been placed in use by some Middle Eastern and nearby nations, but not in far flung Islam.

The Hanifa school of jurisprudences is said to be the most tolerant. The Maliki are said to follow existing local legal practices. The Shafi focus on the hadiths but also used analogy and reason, while the Hanbali stick to the literal hadiths. This words mean little, the important point being that all use their own "interpretations" of the Koran, which itself is in conflict with the Koran.

Jafar al-Sadiq (d765) established a fifth school of jurisprudence, this one being Shiite, with an Imam that effectively represents a religious hierarchy with authority of interpretation. The other four schools of jurisprudence are Sunni and are said to argue more over matters of authority and compete with one another in interpreting the "laws" they basically wrote. The Shiite and their Sufi outgrowth were considered extremists or outcasts by the Sunni *ulama*. The Sunni oppressed and murdered Shiite, and the Shiite reciprocated when they could.

Perhaps the most famous, or infamous, of the extremists was Ibn Taymiyyah (1263-1328) a Hanbali who set the pattern for domination by pushing the Shariah as the instrument of extremist control of the secular. Again, believers were labeled unbelievers in the tradition of Kharijite, but now there was something in hand to use as a weapon, the Shariah. Taymiyyah would say that a person who does not accept the Shariah is not a Muslim. The Shariah replaced the Koran as a source of authority; the man-made replaced the divine. The views of Taymiyyah became more important to extremists than the words of Allah.

All that followed in time were largely variations on the theme, although the Wahhabi may have cut some new ground. Muhammad Ibn Abd al-Wahhab (1703-1792) started proselytizing his extreme version of Islam in 1740, raising the ire of his own family members due to its heretofore unexpressed theories. The Wahhabi destroyed religious sites, dug up graves, burned books, rigidly labeled Muslims as non-believers for not praying on time all the time, and condemned music. They felt that Muhammad was being worshipped, which would be against the dictates of Islam, and destroyed his gravesite. Or so it was said.

To the extent there is animosity between Saudi Arabia and Iran, it might have been attributable more to the Wahhabi than the traditional Sunni and Shiite split dating back over a thousand years, Saudi Arabia represented the Sunni, and Iran the Shiite. In the early 19th century, the Wahhabi effectively repeated the earlier atrocities against Hussein (Ali's heir) in attacking and destroying Hussein's tomb and shrine in the city of Karbala, Iraq, a Shiite stronghold near Iran. The Wahhabi, then being the religious partners of the House of Saud, had thus made a very aggressive move against the Shiite in Iraq and Iran.

A string of extremists and terrorists followed, with Osama bin-Laden being the current version. All disobey the Koran, and yet Islam has not been able to rid itself of such extremism even though it has tried to do so.

The history of extremism in Islam was much more extensive than I have covered here. Although the extremists and the extremist groups vary quite a bit, they all express their own views and vie for acceptance by other Muslims. Some become terrorists and try to impose their views on others. Some just advance their own views and foment trouble in the land, perhaps as a means to get attention and influence.

There were so many noted extremists, usually based on writing some noted commentary, over the centuries that it almost seems like a tradition of extremism exists in Islam. But it is not that because the extremists have different views and different agendas. If a common denominator exists, it would seem to be the striving for personal influence through notoriety.

I, for one, believe this as I feel that the Koran is so clear that the extremists cannot really believe the contradictions of the Koran that they advance. Based on this, I feel that their positions must be derived with non-religious purposes in mind, namely seeking influence.

Chapter Six

# The *Ulama*

In ancient days the *ulama* sought to dominate Islam. They were the learned, the schooled, the doctors of jurisprudence who were without a franchise, caught between a caliph who had the political power and a growing leaderless religion. War was the best game in town, as it had been for millennia in Arabia, but that was not for the learned.

Exactly what happened is not actually known as there is no written, archeological, or scientific evidence to lay out the story of this early time. Many portrayals exist. This is the story I build from what I have read.

They *ulama* came into their own soon after the death of Muhammad in 632. Somebody had to compile the Koran under the command of the caliph who ordered it done, and that would naturally fall to the learned of the community. The *ulama* did the job, probably restrained from incorporating too many of their own views into the process because they were dealing largely with oral recollections of people who were actually there or not far removed from those hearing Muhammad recite the words of Allah. Also, the *ulama's* personal views probably weren't yet mature as Islam was so new and the Koran hadn't yet been compiled. There was no book and few were likely to have known the full gamut of Muhammad's recitals.

The Koran was complete and final about say 650 and it still wasn't decided how the Caliphate should wear the religious hat. Muhammad had been both the secular and religious ruler, providing precedent for that. There was also enough other precedent for a secular ruler, be it a tribal leader or a king, or in those days a caliph or sultan. There was no precedent for a religious leader other than Muhammad himself, and he was the last of the prophets (33.40).

Islam was new to the scene and the Koran said nothing about a religious hierarchy. Furthermore, the Koran could be viewed as denying or barring both a religious hierarchy or any intermediary to Allah as each believer was to have his or own personal and direct relationship with Allah.

The *ulama* first interjected themselves as the intermediary between the caliph and the people. The political decision reached by the political power base including the caliph was that, on religious matters, the caliph was to consult the community of believers and achieve agreement or consensus. Whether this consultative process became unwieldy or whether the *ulama* just used influence or the power of "learned" criticism, the *ulama* essentially inserted themselves as the representative of the general community in providing the community religious confirmation to the caliphs.

As is normal the case in elite relationships, and there being no reason to believe it wasn't also the case in ancient days, it probably got to the point where the Caliphate and the *ulama* helped each other by working hand-in-hand with both parties made to look good in the process. By doing so, both were able to consolidate and advance their positions.

But only too soon the *ulama* split into groups or sects of like-minded individuals. For some reason, perhaps just human nature, the *ulama* just could not coalesce and agree amongst themselves. Some in those sects became extremists who rebelled, murdered and sought dominance in one fashion of another. That was one of the ways to power and influence in an age that didn't have too many ways for a man to distinguish himself. The age of the extremists had arisen. That took place by 660, when what might be called the first terrorist sect, the Kharijite, murdered the fourth and last caliph, Ali.

It was another 200 years or so before the hadiths were compiled, and by that time the various *ulama* sects were

well established, each pursuing their own group ideology
and agenda. Perhaps more so than is the case with others,
the learned have a wide range of personal views and are not
the most likely to yield to one another. They established
any number of schools of jurisprudence; that is, schools of
Koranic interpretation. Eventually it resolved down to four
major schools of jurisprudence and, when they finished
compiling the hadiths, each school had their own set of
hadiths. That was about the middle of the 9th century.

The Shariah, evolving out of the hadiths, covered most
every aspect of secular society including such matters as to
how to trim one's beard. The *ulama*, authors of the Shariah
just as they had been the authors of the hadiths, could
include what they wanted. No one was around from the
time of Muhammad to correct them. Although oral
tradition was still strong, the passage of time dulled it,
limiting the remaining restraint on the *ulama*. In the
following centuries, splinter groups of *ulama* established
still more sects.


## THE *ULAMA* DEVELOPES TO INCLUDE A CLERGY

Some have said that the *ulama* or learned ones were
those who had special knowledge of the religion. It
probably didn't start that way. The learned were called to
compile the Koran because they were the educated who
could read and write, not necessarily because of any special

knowledge of religion. Islam wasn't fully established at the time Muhammad died nor a few years later when Umar started the compilation effort.

By the time the hadiths and the Shariah were written, Islam was well established and prosperous. Prosperity brought more personal leisure, more education and more learned who knew the Koran. Islam branched out on all fronts.

Somewhere along the line, what is today called mosques started to proliferate. Mosques probably grew out of gatherings of the faithful in the open near Muhammad, his home or wherever he tended to be. Structures sprung up and undoubtedly became good places for believers to congregate and pray. In time, somebody was selected to lead the prayers, most probably from the learned *ulama*, and imams came on the scene.

An imam is the person *who stands in front*, essentially the leader of the congregation. At first they were mere leaders in prayer, which might not have required the truly learned. But that would have changed in time as they did became more learned and made themselves into full fledged clerics with their own self-appointed hierarchies.

The *ulama*, including and cleric contingent, expanded the scope of their activities. Religious schools were formed and the scholars, including the learned clerics, became the teachers.    Scholarship   thrived   and   scholarly   texts proliferated.  The scholars started to compete, as scholars everywhere are prone to do.   Naturally, the competition was not physical, and probably not financially driven, at least initially.  It was a competition of ideas, thoughts, and "interpretations,"   all   within   the   religious   area.    Like everything else, there were probably variations in piousness and in self-interest that entered into the completion for the minds of the believers.

Both the *ulama* and the clergy grew exponentially, evolving into more structured groups and finding means of economic support.  The Koran called for aiding the poor through   charity   and   the   strong   Muslim   tradition   of charitable giving came to embrace support of the *ulama* and the clergy, frequently as teachers and likely as the administrators of the charitable giving when it went beyond arms to the poor on the street corner.

Just like the rest of the *ulama*, the clerics were of all persuasions.  Some stuck to leading prayers, some provided what might seem similar to righteous sermons, particularly on  Friday  nights,  and  some  have  obviously  become firebrands, exhorting listeners to most violent behavior.

Whether by deliberation or true piousness, the *ulama* and the clerics expanded their scope and eventually began to compete  with  the  state  ruler  for  overall  dominance. Every step along the way, the *ulama* and the clerics had accreted power and control to themselves. A great variation in religious views developed over time within both the *ulama* and the clergy, leading to competition between themselves for dominance over the other as well as competition with the state ruler for dominance over the people.

The extremists amongst them created hostility and hatred amongst segments of the society, resulting in some Muslims even calling other Muslims barbarians. In the process, ordinary Muslims were being marginalized, if not killed.

## THE KORAN DOES NOT FAVOR A CLERGY

The Koran has a number of passages that speak out against a clergy. Doctors of laws, priests and monks, the terms used in the Koran to refer to those who deal primarily with religion, are not favored by the plain words of the Koran and can hardly be used to justify existence of a clergy or the existence of any sort of religious hierarchy.

Different robes do not matter as the Koran lumps them all together. So-called clergymen can give wrong religious advice contrary to the commands of Allah, and yet the public might believe they have authority to do what they do. The Koran wants Muslims to focus on what it says and not on what the scholars, jurists and others say:

*The Koran was sent to you explained in full detail (6.114).*
*Do not take the doctors of law and the very pious as you*
*would your Lord (9.31).*
*Do not sanctimoniously claim to be guided by Allah.*
*Allah chooses to guide whom He will (4.49).*
*Allah has no partner (4.48).*

The Koran is particularly adverse to the super-pious that it calls monks. Muslims are cautioned about their connections with the doctors of law, rabbis, priests and those who are ultra-dedicated:

*Pious monastic life is the innovation of others, not Allah.*
*Allah requires only that believers please Him by right*
*observance (57.27).*
*Beware of the doctors of law and the very pious who*
*falsely waste your charity and deprive you of funds*
*for true charity in Allah's way (9.34).*

## THE TWO-SIDED CONFLICT WITH THE *ULAMA*

A secular Muslim society has the ability to turn the situation around on the extremist *ulama* and clergy, and incidentally do in the rest of the *ulama*. Turkey had done just that decades ago and presently seems to be moving back toward moderation.

When Mustafah Kemal Ataturk created the secular Turkish state some eighty years ago, he aimed to demolish the extremist *ulama* that endangered the type of society he wanted. Rule making authority was taken away from the *ulama* and it was stripped of judicial authority. Ataturk had the state take over the educational function, so frequently run by the *ulama* in Muslim counties. He eliminated the charitable endowments that supported the *ulama*, compounding the financial disaster. With the loss of power and financial support, the entire *ulama* were marginalized. The ordinary Muslim community was restored to power.

The firebrand clerics and those of like mind are most active in trying to get Muslim nations to adopt the Shariah for that would give the firebrands the political power they obviously seek. Yet, where they have been successful, the results have been dire, as witness the killings, oppression and persecution in the countries they control. The Taliban in Afghanistan provided a prime example.

On the other side of the coin, the extremist *ulama* have also been persecuted and murdered, and the killing probably included some of the *ulama* who aren't extremists. Where the extremists have lost their struggle, they could be slaughtered on a very large scale, as was the case in Ataturk's Turkey, Nasser's Egypt and Assad's Syria.

Battles used to be fought with arms, but lately started to be fought at the ballot box. In a corrupt country where a robust *ulama* provides much in social services and personal aid to the population, the extremist *ulama* could win at the ballot box. But with such extremists, a fear arises that it might turn out to be one person one vote, but only one time before elections are eliminated.

The problem with free elections is that the extremist *ulama* do not believe in them as they are the ones that took from the community of ordinary Muslims the power the Koran conferred on them. The extremists are not likely to give that power back if they lose an election after having won one. Thus the likelihood exists that there would no longer be free elections once the extremists won at the ballot box. Yet the Koran does stand for the community reaching a consensus and thus would favor the use of the ballot box.

## LIVE AND LET LIVE?

One cannot really take issue with people of like -mind adopting the Shariah for themselves. It is the insistence that others also adhere to the Shariah that creates disagreement and conflict. There doesn't seem to be any reason why a Muslim society couldn't allow a segment of their society to live under the Shariah if it is voluntary.

Examples of something like this abound in the world. Such an arrangement was found in Islam's history as that was the way the ancient Arabs treated the *dhimmi* who lived amongst or near them. The *dhimmi* had religious freedom and lived under their own laws administered by their own leaders under the protection of the Arabs. Another example would be the Ottoman administering a huge Islamic empire and recognizing *milletler* or *millets*, which were basically nations-within-nations, set up along religious lines.

Examples also exist in the West. The most telling examples happen to be in the United States where the Indian tribes are recognized as nations, with some sovereign rights. Also the Amish Christians in the United States live in accordance with their own religious dictates and use the ancient ways for themselves although they are not quite separate and apart from the rest of society. The Amish congregate together in areas considered theirs but not exclusively so as they live amongst others. The Indian tribes live on lands that are theirs.

The Amish shun modernity, use no electricity and use horses instead of autos. The to-be-expected road friction between a horse-drawn society and a high-speed automotive society seems to be kept in bounds. They also have their own schools and basically get no special support from the state.

An important feature about the way this works in the United States is that any member of an Indian tribe or the Amish society is free to leave the tribe or the society and join other Americans anywhere they want. It is all voluntary, at all times.

A society-within-a-society would appear to be consistent with the Koran which recognizes the existence of separate nations, tribes and peoples.

Thus, a group adopting the Shariah for itself in a given area as a personal lifestyle matter could be a way to avoid conflict if the majority would allow it on a voluntary basis. If that would not satisfy those who seek to live under Shariah, their purpose in attempting to impose Shariah on the entire society would be shown to be political, not pious.

## THE *ULAMA'S* RESTRICTIVE INFLUENCE

Except in rare instances, the theological dogma of the *ulama* tends to be restrictive, not freeing.  It is restrictive, not in any pejorative sense of being bad, but rather that it limits or curtails possible human activity, it directs time and effort, or it increases punishments.  Over time, such restrictive views have found their way into Muslim society. The dress code for women would be an example.  One might question whether such restrictions were called-for, necessary or useful, or even whether they violate the Koran.  However, the pattern was clear -- the religion had gotten more restrictive with the passage of time, until very recently.

Islam spread widely and quickly during and following Muhammad's life.  It was during the 200 years or so following Muhammad's death that Islam started to become "the light of the world." Islam advanced much further in the sciences and the arts than Christian Europe or anywhere else. For a while, Islam was the world leader in intellectual and scientific achievement. Islam preserved the ancient wisdom of the Greeks and added to knowledge in all fields.

The *dhimma* system helped by providing people who could translate Western texts into Arabic. The Christians and Jews living in a tolerant Islam were not adverse to traveling to "barbarian" lands to learn the new languages and tapping for Islam the then existing Western advances. The Islamic religion nourished and freed the Muslim mind and Islam advanced beyond any other civilization.

The world suffered a great loss when Islam ceased being the light of the world. The *ulama's* growing restrictiveness was creating an ever more oppressive Islamic society. After the fall of the Roman Empire, the West entered the dark ages. For a couple of centuries Islam was the light of the world and then the accumulated weight of *ulama* driven repression and oppression took hold and inhibited Islamic society. Islam began to fall by the wayside intellectually and scientifically, although the religion continued to spread in far flung places.

The subsequent advances in the West wouldn't have meant much comparatively if Islam had continued its own advances -- but Islam did not continue to advance. In about the 10<sup>th</sup> century, the advances stopped and regression started to set in. Thereafter, for centuries, Islam seemed to have been left behind in sort of a time warp.

The "decline and fall" of Islam from its height as the light of the world could be ascribed to another aspect of society aside from, or in addition to, the increasing repression by a strengthening *ulama*. Much could be ascribed to the personal extravagance, debauchery and decadence of the caliphs. But still it would be difficult to ignore, for instance, that, by 935, members of the Hanbali school of jurisprudence were raiding houses to check compliance with the laws of Islam, their laws. So at this point, there are two possible explanations for the decline: the growing debauchery and the growing restrictive orthodoxy.

There is no definitive work like the "Decline and Fall of the Roman Empire" by Gibbons that would explain what happened on the intellectual and scientific end as Islam became the light of the world and then declimed. Islam itself has directed blame to foreigners; at first the Mongols, then the Turks (actually there was a renaissance under the Turks), and later blamed the British and French. The blame, it seems, could well rest with the extremist fringe of the *ulama*.

## HOW CAN ALL THIS HAPPEN IN DISOBEDIENCE TO THE KORAN?

A Westerner has to wonder how the disconnections with the Korans can happen. A plain reading of the words of the Koran clearly shows the extremist segment of the *ulama* to have disobeyed, disregarded and dishonored the Koran, and yet they continue to profess that they are good Muslims or even that they are the only true Muslims. The disconnects between the dictates of the religion and the actions of some in the *ulama* are too great and too obvious to ignore.

The Koran says it explains everything, and the *ulama* have many schools of jurisprudence to explain otherwise. The Koran say that Muslims should not form sects, and the *ulama* does so. The Koran provides for no religious hierarchy and the *ulama* creates them. The Koran says that Allah has no partner and the *ulama* create a clergy to do just that. The Koran recognizes the secular state and some in the *ulama* would obliterate it. The Koran says a Muslim cannot fight and kill without being attacked first and the extremist *ulama* say they can. The Koran says be kind to Jews and Christians while the firebrand *ulama* does the opposite. And there is much, much more. How does it happen?

One could say that it is due either the absence of an authorized religious hierarchy to control matters, or that ordinary Muslims and the other *ulama* allow it to happen. But these points go to the issue of controlling the extremist *ulama* and not to their mindset in feeling that they have the right to do what they do in opposition to the plain words of the Koran. Would not a true believer feel obliged to follow the Koran? This I find to be inexplicable.

Chapter Seven

# Fighting Back

A basic obligation placed by the Koran on Muslims is to fight back when attacked, which is an appropriate corollary to the Koran being most peaceful and compassionate. It is one thing to be peace loving, as the Koran is, but another to take abuse without fighting back. The words of the Koran are rough and tough when it comes to Muslim fighting back, while taking care to tell Muslims not to be excessive.

That has been seen in the permission Allah gave Muslims to fight and kill only if they were attacked first. When attacked, Muslims are directed to be fierce. The Koran uses rough but realistic language like ambushing and slaying the attackers wherever you find them (9.5), which is what any army anywhere would do. Allah wants Muslims to fight back, but only in the prescribed way, in Allah's way:

*Allah permits Muslins to fight if war is first made on them (22.39).*

*Fight in the way of Allah those who fight against you, but
do not begin the hostilities. Allah does not love
aggressors (2.190).*
*Do not flee before unbelievers marching against you in
war (8.15).*
*Use whatever force you can muster and all your strength
against your enemy in war to strike fear into them
(8.60).*
*When you retaliate, retaliate no worse than the fashion
you were confronted with (16.126).*
*Give as you get; attack in the manner you were attacked
(2.194).*

The theme of giving as you get expands into the
concept of a law of equality or retribution. Parity is sought,
escalation shunned, and the parity requirement might be
cast in different ways. It might merely be tit for tat, of like-
kind. Or it might be the transfer of burdens. It is as wrong
to fight back excessively, to exceed the limits, as it is not to
fight back at all. Islam stands for balance.

If you help an evil cause, you will bear the burdens of
it. If you mislead persons who are not knowledgeable or
can't take care of themselves, the law of equality requires
you to bear the evil burdens you created by misleading.
The punishment or retaliation for killing a believer, which
includes Jews and Christians as well as Muslims, depends
on whether it is intentional. Equity, right and compassion
are all rolled into Islam's required balance:

*A believer should not kill a believer unless it is by mistake,
in which case compensation is payable (4.92).*

*Allah curses, and punishes with hell, whoever intentionally kills a believer (4.93).*

*Under the law of equality, the retaliation prescribed for murder is death for death; but if instead requested by the victim's brother, compensation is payable (2.178-179).*

*Everyone will bear their own evil burdens in full on the day of judgment, and also the evil burdens of any unknowledgeable people they misled (16.25).*

*Whoever helps a good cause will have its reward and whoever helps an evil cause will bear the burdens of it (4.85).*

The Koran clearly wants people to live in peace. That is even more important than spreading the religion, a primary goal of many religions. The Koran says proselytize, but do not use force and walk away when denied. The overriding concern does appear to be peace. Again, Allah wants Muslims to fight back or go forth in His way, either way as the case may be, but in all events balance is required. We've seen these verses before, but they are worth repeating in this context:

*There should be no compulsion in religion (2.256).*

*Invite all to the way of Allah using reason and beautiful preaching, and graciously convince them using your best approach (16.125).*

*If the People of the Book and the unlearned people turn their backs on submitting to Islam, your duty is only to have delivered the message (3.20).*

*Allah requires that you respect, show kindness and deal justly with those who do not fight with you for religion or drive you from your homes (60.8).*

Muslims have a duty to fight back when attacked, but there is one situation where Muslims have to fight but not in the context of fighting back. Muslims have an affirmative duty to fight other Muslims who are creating conflict. Even when they are not attacked, if Muslims are quarreling, other Muslims have a duty to make peace, and failing that, fight the wrongdoer. Peace amongst Muslims is so important to Allah that He authorized fighting to achieve it without having been attacked first:

*All believers are brethren and you have a duty to make peace between your contending brethren (49.10).*

*If parties of believers quarrel, make peace between them with fairness and justice. If one party does wrong to the other, fight the one who does wrong until they obey Allah (49.9).*

In a sense, Allah is setting a higher standard for Muslims vis a vis fellow believers as compared to non-believers. The duty is to fight back when non-believers attack first. The duty is to fight other believers when they refuse to stop quarrelling; that is, to fight other believers even when not attacked by them, depending on the circumstances. Allah wants peace amongst Muslims and that is important enough for Him to condone fighting to stop Muslims from quarreling with each other. And even then, Allah shows his commitment to peace by first requiring that an attempt be made to bring peace by the use of peaceful means. Only when peace cannot be achieved through peaceful means does Allah require fighting, against the wrongdoer.

What is doing wrong? That too is made clear by the Koran. Disobeying the Koran is wrong. Disobeying Allah is wrong:

*The revelations of the Koran are from Allah (46.2)*
*Muslims who disobey Allah should fear the retribution of a grievous day (6.15).*
*Obey Allah and do not enter into disputes with one another (8.46).*
*Obey Allah and those in authority among you (4.59).*

Muslins are "required to punish any fellow Muslims who violate Islamic teachings" according to the imam of the Prophet Mosque in Medina[4]. This statement was made in the context of punishing those who killed 34 Saudis, Americans and others by bombing three residential compounds in the Saudi capital in 2003. The imam of the Grand Mosque in Mecca condemned the bombings as "criminal acts" and "an aggression, an act of killing, terrorizing others and destruction," as well as "bloodshed of protected souls."[5]

Muslims are instructed by the Koran to get involved where Muslims fight Muslims. They are instructed to bring peace one way or the other -- either convince the group of

---

[4] Statement of the imam Ali bin Abdel Rahman al-Hudhaify as quoted in *Suicide Bombings Are Condemned in Saudi Mosques*, by Steven R. Weisman, The New York Times, May 17, 2003.
[5] Ibid, statement of the imam Sheik Saleh bin Abdullah bin Humaid.

wrongdoers to stop fighting or join in fighting against the wrongdoers. It does not appear optional as the Koran speaks in terms of duty.


## CLERICS ARE NOT EXEMPT FROM PUNISHMENT

A cleric has no special status. As we have seen, the Koran points to Muhammad as a mortal man (17.93), and a cleric should not be able to claim more. A cleric is subject to Allah's judgment on judgment day as are all other men. There is neither a grant of any special authority to a cleric nor any grant of infallibility to a cleric. While Muslims should obey Allah and those who govern them (4.58-59), there is no requirement to obey clerics.

I use the term "clerics" to include mullahs, imams, ayatollahs and those who have other names connoting religious authority even though no such authority is actually granted in the Koran. Islam does not have a religious hierarchy as is found in the West, as for instance in the Catholic Church with a pope, cardinals, bishops and others.

An imam is a leader in prayer at a mosque, a mullah is a Moslem teacher of the sacred law, and an ayatollah is a term used by the Shiite indicating a cleric with advanced knowledge of Islamic law. Ordinary Muslims accept their positions and listen when they give sermons or talks. The ayatollahs have some derived authority from the Imam the Shiites believe in, and an ayatollah is presently the effective head of state in Iran.

I use the term "firebrand cleric" as one who exhorts, kindles or encourages extremist-terrorist activity amongst the ordinary Muslims they preach to. The cleric's exhortations might be very direct, using words like "kill" or "throw bombs." Or the exhortation could be indirect and even vague and yet the cleric's motive and intent to incite can be clear.

Because of his knowledge and respected position in society, the cleric is considered a religious leader and his words carry weight notwithstanding the technical absence of authority. But still, the Koran doesn't have kind words about the learned doctors of laws and the very pious, and Allah claims no partner:

*Do not take the doctors of laws and the very pious as you would your Lord (9.31).*
*Beware of the doctors of law and the very pious who falsely waste your charity and deprive you of funds for true charity in Allah's way (9.34).*
*Allah has no partner (4.48).*

As Muhammad might encounter personal adversity (7.188), so might a mere cleric. The cleric is clearly not untouchable. Like all other men, the cleric is responsible for what he does. More so, he is also responsible if he misleads others not as learned as he is (16.25). As he is responsible for his actions, it should surely follow that he can be punished by Allah if he strays. The state certainly has the power to punish for disobedience of its laws. And the Koran instructs Muslims to fight the Muslim wrongdoer when Muslim quarrel or fight other Muslims. Ordinary Muslims joining the fight against those who caused the suicide bombings in Saudi Arabia would be justified.

Once the wrongdoers cease fighting, if that can be determined, those who are fighting them should also cease:

*If the enemy who attacked you ceases to fight against you, you should also cease fighting (2.192).*
*Desist from fighting the enemy if the enemy desists; return to fighting if the enemy returns to the attack(8.19).*
*If the enemy is inclined to peace, you should also be inclined to peace (8.61).*

Muslims have the duty to discuss and decide things amongst themselves (42.38). As the Koran has given nobody religious authority over others, a cleric has just as much authority as the ordinary Muslims choose to give them. An ordinary Muslim who knows the Koran can be considered as "learned" as a cleric might be, and have the same right to speak out. Speaking-out against "any fellow Muslims who violate Islamic teachings," as the imam said, would be a form of fighting them, if not punishing them. Muslims could confront the firebrand clerics in a war of words.

## FIGHTING BACK

From the outside, it seems that the silent majority of Muslims do not counter the extremist-terrorists who threaten to destroy their way of life. If the extremist-terrorists were ever successful, a Taliban type society would likely be imposed on the ordinary, silent Muslims. It may be that the ordinary Muslims are relying on their secular governments (as representing the required Koranic community consensus) to find, apprehend and punish legal wrongdoers, but government enforcement goes only so far.

A battle for minds is also being fought, and here ordinary Muslims are free under the Koran to do what they will. The Koran grants no special authority and no religious authority to any Muslim over any other Muslim, and knowledgeable Muslims are free to voice their opinions in opposition to whomever they wish, including the firebrand clerics. It would seem that ordinary Muslims could properly enter into the battle to form public opinion, but it seems that they do not. Why is this? Perhaps they are being cowed into silence.

Cowed, but certainly not cowards. Something else seems to be at work here. Perhaps it is something as simple as Muslims not believing that they are the true targets of the extremist-terrorists, it being camouflaged by all the rhetoric being directed against the West, against America and against the Jews. However, if one looks to history as

143

well as current events, it does appear that the true targets of the extremist-terrorists have always been the secular Muslims and the secular Muslim states.

What is happening today seems no different. The basic attack is on the secular society, the modern secular society most Muslims live in. Should the silent majority of ordinary Muslims become aware that they are the true targets of the extremist clerics, they could not be cowed into silence.

# Chapter Eight

# The Disconnect

The history of Islam and the writings of centuries of *ulama* confirm the existence of vast disconnects between the Koran and actual practice of the religion, as if we needed that confirmation by now. However, it also confirms that the disconnects are not isolated, occasional occurrences happening now and then. Rather, the disconnects represent a continuing undercurrent of what the Koran would call trouble making in the land.

To be sure, Judaism and Christianity faced theological differences amongst the faithful over the centuries, as shown by their being split up into denominations; a multitude of them in the case of Christianity. However, comparative religion can yield nothing because religion is a matter of faith and there is no way to evaluate or compare faiths.

In my view, the Koranic disconnects do not grow out the theology of the religion. The theology of the Koran is clear enough, surprisingly clear, so different theological readings could not reasonably be at the core of the disconnects. I am convinced that the disconnects arise from the entire gamut of personal human motivations, with the religious or theological rationales being just fabrications. Thus, I find it understandable that believers were not able to find ways to irradicate the disconnects although I am sure that many tried over the centuries.

The same personal human motivations (e.g. power) kept the differing groups of *ulama* from striving to coalesce or to get together to solve the problems their societies face. They need to continue to maintain their rationales, differences, positions, and agendas. In a sense, they cannot afford to solve the societal problems, even if they could do so, because their very rationale would disappear.

The only real changes over the centuries were in who or what the extremist *ulama* blame or attack in the process of advancing their positions, each picking an appropriate enemy to have at the time. Right now that is Israel and the West, with the United States representing the West. Ordinary Muslim need not agree with them. For instance, it has been shown again and again that the people might like or respect the United States. But that does not matter for the extremist *ulama* must have a foe.

In ancient days, the foe would have been other Muslims for there was then no one else to oppose. Thus,

146

those Muslims who played music or showed respect at Muhammad's grave became the foe as facilitating religious positions arose, damning music or deeming Muhammad's grave a place of worship forbidden in Islam. Today, the deliberate killing of other Muslims and the destruction of Islamic holy sites seem to have stopped, and the focus broadened because the world focus expanded. Now blame is cast upon others grounded upon current issues and circumstances.

For what it is worth, I explore some of the current blame rationalizations being cast about:

**Globalization.** Some *ulama* blame much on the West because of globalization, a popular but empty refrain. The argument is easily discredited by considering how much Malaysia, an Islamic country, has benefited from modern globalization. Malaysia is thriving superbly by both Islamic and Western standards.

Islam can and does benefit from globalization as the global markets supply goods and services to Islam and allow Islam to sell its goods around the globe. The primary export of the Islamic countries in the Middle East is oil, while other Islamic countries are more diversified, but not as wealthy.

Some commentators say that the oil wealth perversely resulted in a lower rate of human resource development in the Middle East than would otherwise have been the case. Their reason is that the oil money was so easy to come by that there was no need to educate and develop the skills of their populations.

Those commentators would point to Malaysia as having developed its human resources because it had little by way of natural resources and, in so doing, achieved greater long-term social benefit. While the argument could have been made decades ago, today it fails as the Middle East is developing itself on many fronts, taking the lead on some fronts. For instance, the biggest buildings and building projects in the world are now in Arabia.

Globalization essentially stands for free trade. Those who can't complete complain about it and find all sorts of reason why it is unfair. Yet, many less developed nations have benefited from it. While Malaysia might be the example chosen because it is an Islamic state, there are also the examples of other Asian and Latin American countries that compete well the global markets. India, with a big Muslim population, benefits from globalization by rendering computer software services into the highly developed United States of all places -- which proves the fact that globalization works both ways, and the dice are not loaded in favor of the West.

**Anti-Islamic.** Another rationale is that the West is out to oppress or oppose Islam, a matter that is clearly denied by the number of times the West has recently gone to war in order to help Muslims. These were not minor, idle gestures but were serious and far reaching, involving the volunteering of both treasure and blood. The West aided the Afghans in their just jihad against the Russians, and went to the aid of Kuwait when it was invaded. To be sure, there were political and economic reasons which coincided, but the fact remains that the West did not act against Muslim interests and was not acting anti-Islam.

The West also went to the aid of Muslims in Kosovo and Bosnia where there were no political or economic reasons that could have possibly prompted that aid. The West has gone to the aid of those Muslims for purely humanitarian reasons, belying the criticism leveled against it. These matters are more fully covered in the Appendix under "*Just and Unjust Jihads.*"

Nor can the establishment of the State of Israel be viewed as anti-Islamic, as the motivation of neither the United Nations nor the United States was anti-Islamic. When the unexpected Palestinian political opposition arose, prompted only by the extremist *ulama* and not the Palestinian people themselves, the United Nations offered to sponsor two nations, again opposed only by the extremists and not the people.

**Supports repressive regimes.** The West had been accused of propping up repressive regimes and there had been some merit in this argument. However, at least with respect to the United States, it is no longer the case. The United States had redefined the way it determines its national interest and now pushes repressive regimes to change their ways.

All that can reasonably be said today is that things progress too slowly. Yet perhaps it remains the better path for more a more aggressive path might create too much trouble in the land, trouble that would be avoided with more gradual progress. Yet the unfortunate part is that as long as the repressive regimes continue to exist, the extremist *ulama* do have their talking points.

**Poverty.** To the extent there is poverty in Islam, it is the likely result of the internal strife in Islam rather than poverty being the cause of that strife. The internal strife of Islam is caused by the extremist *ulama*, and it appears in the wealthier as well as the poorer Islamic nations.

Nor can it be said that Islam is impoverished in any sense of the word. There is substantial wealth in the Islamic Middle East, with only pockets of poverty. The Middle East has both capital wealth and capable people, and yet something keeps it from putting it all together, with the extremist *ulama* seeming to be that "something."

**Repression.** It is not clear how the supposed repression of Islam takes place. For example, assume the so-called export of Western culture is the claimed culprit. If that is it, Islam must be unique in some unidentified way since others do not feel that they were being repressed by exported Western culture, or any other culture. Besides, there is doubt that a culture can be exported as contrasted to it being imported by those who want to share in it. Culture, like religion, cannot be forced on others;  it is voluntarily absorbed only if it is liked. Rather, Western culture seems to be opposed by those of the *ulama* who oppose all secular cultures.

Somehow the West is blamed for repressing Islam, whereas the extremist *ulama* is the true cause of repression in Islam as it has been in the past. It was the restrictiveness and repression of the *ulama* which caused Islam to lose its leadership in the arts and sciences a thousand years ago, and those of like-mind effectively restrain Islam from making significant contributions today.

**Humiliation.**  Talk about humiliation leads nowhere and is generally specious, except that the extremists find it a useful tool in fomenting loss of self-esteem and discontent.  The talk about Muslims being humiliated and having lost their self-esteem because of the West never presents any rationale in support.  The super-achieving Malaysia should belie any reason for Muslim humiliation. Yet the extremist *ulama*, and they alone, seem to pound on allegations of humiliation so as to introduce a dysfunctional element into the secular societies they oppose.

**Spirituality.** The West is criticized for its lack of spirituality and its concentration on materiality, with the prime example said to be the United States. While there are no standards for measuring spirituality, there are statistics that shows the United States as being one of the most church-going nations.

But it is essentially impossible to compare religions in terms of spirituality which have many forms of expression. Yet the extremist *ulama* feel that they can criticize the West for a lack of spirituality as they continue to disregard the plain words of their own Scripture.

## WHAT HAPPENS NOW?

The community of ordinary Muslims has always been on the receiving end of extremist *ulama* excesses. Yet, ordinary Muslims, like people everywhere, tend to avoid contentious matters, reflecting a reluctance to *rock the boat* if they can *live with it*. While Muslims are very polite, it cannot be said that they are too polite to correct someone who is stepping on their toes. They can act in a politically and religiously acceptable fashion if they wish to correct others. They know that leaving issues unresolved can come back to harm them and their children as well. And their Koran gives them an affirmative duty to settle clashes amongst Muslims, including those created by the extremists.

The underlying issue in Islam may be one of lifestyle. As longs as the extremist *ulama* try to impose their views on others, ordinary Muslims will have to resist or find their way of life changed.  The extremist *ulama* empower themselves, and their cadres expand day-to-day as they openly train and develop their followers, but the silent majority of ordinary Muslims tend to remain silent. Ordinary Muslims have so far been able to *live with it.*

The bombings in Saudi Arabia were one of many wake up calls.  The issue had been drawn in such a way that the lifestyle of ordinary Muslims must change one way or the other:  either they actively enter the fray to make peace and fight the wrongdoer as the Koran demands, or they await the lifestyle change as the extremist *ulama* take over. Either way, life can no longer remain the same  --  the extremist *ulama* have forced the issue.

The Koranic dictate is to give back what you get (2.194), and fighting back against the extremists would be both just and required.  Giving back what you get is largely tit-for-tat, doing what is done to you.  If they rant and rave, it would seem that ordinary Muslims would be justified, or commanded, to rant and rave back at the same time and place.  They could respond to false rhetoric with corrective rhetoric, and not just ignore the false rhetoric.  If ordinary Muslims are labeled barbarians or non-Muslims, so should they call their assailants under the laws of equality and retaliation.  All this is in the plain reading of the Koran.

If pebbles or stones are cast, so should they be cast in retaliation, but, when it comes to physical action, the Koran calls for group action. In the modern context that might mean also eliciting assistance from the local authorities who represent the community.

The Koranic instruction to fight all together demands united action or a consensus to fight. Either way, it stands for the unity amongst Muslims that Islam strives for. Making peace amongst quarrelling Muslims (49.9-10) is part of it this. So too the command not to split up into sects (6.159). The requirement to fight all together also shows that there is no individual duty to fight. Extremists invariably lack the required community consensus.

Perhaps the best approach to combat the extremists is to read the Koran itself and take the time to understand. It seems that too many people in all religions recite but do not understand. And too many rely on what others tell them and do not themselves read the Scriptures. The Koran recognizes this:

*Those who lack knowledge and understanding know the Scripture only through hearsay and do nothing but guess (2.78).*

It does seem that the rock of Islam is the Koran, standing eternally with its very plain language awaiting for it to be read, understood and followed and, with that, eradicate the disconnects.

Appendix 1

# Advice to Would-Be Jihadists

> This is addressed to young Muslims who may be thinking about joining an extremist jihad.
>
> Westerners should also read this in order to understand more about the jihads and the afterlife.
>
> Jihad means striving hard in the way of Allah, which can include anything between personal self-improvement and killing others, depending on the circumstances and Koranic dictates.

No matter what you have been told by others, the Koran makes you personally responsible for deciding to join a jihad that is not in the way of Allah. Allah was aware that some Muslims misrepresent things, so Allah issued a Koranic warning to all Muslims to be beware of this. So you should recognize the possibility that you are being misled -- Allah said so. The "unknowledgeable" Allah refers to would include those people, probably very much like you, who would ordinarily accept what they are

told without checking it out in the Koran. Allah warns you
that other Muslims can be deceptive:

*There are those whose speech pleases you and who call to
Allah to witness what is in their hearts, yet they are
your deadly enemies (2.204).*

*On judgment day, the command judgment shall be
entirely Allah's and no person shall have power to do
anything for another person (82.19).*

*Everyone will bear their own evil burdens in full on the
day of judgment, and also the evil burdens of any
unknowledgeable people they misled (16.25).*

*Whoever helps a good cause will have its reward and
whoever helps an evil cause will bear the burdens of
it (4.85).*

## CHECK THE KORAN BEFORE YOU JOIN UP

The place to check out what you've been told is the
Koran. Allah said that the Koran covers all things, and He
forbids anybody to add or subtract from it. As the Koran
already covers everything, you need no other references.
Besides, only the Koran is divine; only it comes from
Allah. Allah forbids you from ignoring any part of what
the Koran says:

*Allah has revealed the Koran to you explaining all things
(16.89).*

*The Koran is a clear statement (3.138).*

*Allah has expounded on everything with distinctive
explanation (17.12).*

*Do not associate with Allah that for which He has given*

*you no authority in His revelations (7.33).*
*Do not alter the words from their context nor neglect a*
*portion of what the Koran says (5.13).*

So whatever you have been told, it amounts to nothing if it is not to be found in the Koran. This should be of importance to you because your serving the jihadist cause might destroy your chances of getting into Paradise, not enhance it:

*If a person comes to you with a report, look carefully into*
*the truth lest you harm someone unawares and*
*afterwards be sorry for your actions (49.6).*
*There are those who know all that you do and write it*
*down (82.10-12).*
*Every man's actions will cling to his neck and Allah will*
*bring his book of account wide open for him to see on*
*the day of judgment (17.13-14).*
*Allah will justly balance a person's good and evil deeds so*
*as to not wrong anyone in the slightest degree on the*
*day of judgment (21.47).*

Your must be especially careful if the jihad is to involve killing.  As you know or should know, Allah created all men.  He shuns the taking of life that He Himself has made sacred.  And He takes the killing of even a single human being very, very seriously:

*Whoever killed a human being (unless as punishment for*
*murder or treason), it shall be as though he slew all*
*mankind;  and whoever saved a life, it shall be as*
*though he saved the lives of all mankind (5.32).*
*You should not take life made sacred by Allah, except by*
*way of Allah's law and justice (6.151).*

157

*Those who should fear penalty on the day of judgment are those who commit adultery, or slay a life made sacred by Allah except in the way of Allah's law and justice, or worship another god (25.68).*

## EXACTLY WHAT IS "JUST" CAUSE FOR A JIHAD?

As you know, the term "jihad" literally means hard "effort" or "striving." Thus, your striving to help the poor would be a jihad and also your effort to become a better Muslim. Anything that is in the cause (or path or way) of Allah deserves mighty effort or a jihad on your part, but first you must be sure that your effort or striving will be in the cause of Allah, within Allah's law and justice. Of course, any cause Allah would have would be a just one, but Allah provides no handy definition in the Koran. He provides examples and instructions.

You must examine the examples in the Koran for that is the only way you can determine whether a particular jihad would be a just cause. Two clear examples are provided. One shows that striving hard in prayer and charity and otherwise excelling in what the Koran asks a Muslim to do would be a just personal jihad. The other clear example relates to fighting and killing in the way of Allah which is expressly limited to fighting in defense of the religion after having been attacked first:

*Strive hard (jihad) in Allah's cause as you ought to strive, establishing regular prayer, giving regular charity,*

*and holding fast to Him (22.78).*
*Fight in the way of Allah those who fight against you, but*
*do not begin the hostilities.  Allah does not love*
*aggressors (2.190).*

Thus, your personal jihad includes striving to excel in adhering to the pillars of Islam, expanding your knowledge and understanding of the Koran, your inviting others to join Islam in the way Allah instructed, and your adhering to entire gamut of Allah's other commands.

As you can see, your fighting jihad would involve the taking of sacred life which is clearly against Allah's way, so you have to be very, very careful.  For Muslims to fight and kill, Allah must give His permission and He did so, reluctantly and only in situations where Muslims were attacked first.  Even the fierce "verse of the sword" (9.5) is followed by an explanation that the pagans attacked first. If Muslims are not being attacked, the Koran forbids fighting, and demands that you act as Muslims should normally act, with kindness and justice:

*Allah permits Muslins to fight if war is first made on them*
*(22.39).*
*Fight and kill pagans wheresoever you find them, seize*
*them as captives, beleaguer them, and lie in wait to*
*ambush them (9.5).  Fight those pagans who violated*
*their oaths, assailed your religion and attacked you*
*first (9.13).*
*Allah requires that you respect, show kindness and deal*
*justly with those who do not fight with you for*
*religion or drive you from your homes (60.8).*

## DON'T ACCEPT A FALSE CAUSE

Thus, without having been attacked first, Muslims do not have Allah's permission to fight and are directed by Allah to behave kindly and deal justly. However, you should be very cautious because some people will try to deceive you into believing that Muslims were attacked first by wrongly claiming that all sorts of thing constitute an attack.

***Believers should keep their duty to Allah by speaking straight words (33.70).***

For instance, the claim has been made that Western music that found its way into Islam was an attack on Islam's culture. Another example would be the building of an airbase in Saudi Arabia, which some extremists falsely claim was an attack even though the Saudi government expressly agreed to its building. Don't be fooled, in Muhammad's time as well as now, an attack involved physical violence and bloodletting.

Besides, dredging up false attacks won't work as you will soon see that the Koran limits Muslims to retaliating only in-kind. If Islam is being attacked by Western music, Muslims would be limited to retaliating with Islamic music.

Most people don't mention Allah's law of equality or retribution which seeks to keep things in balance, to even things up instead of escalating them.

## MUSLIMS ARE LIMITED TO RETALIATION IN KIND

Allah's reluctance to condone fighting and killing are reflected in a number of ways in the Koran. Where Muslims are attack first and are allowed to fight back, Allah demands they stop fighting the moment the attackers desist fighting, and Allah also bars Muslims from escalating the fighting by limiting the Muslim to giving back only what they get:

*Desist from fighting the enemy if the enemy desists; return to fighting if the enemy returns to the attack (8.19).*

*Give as you get; attack in the manner you were attacked (2.194).*

*When you retaliate, retaliate no worse than the fashion you were confronted with (16.126).*

Allah's way should be clear to you by now. Allah's compassion is shown by His being against the taking of sacred life except in the exceptional circumstance of Muslims being attacked first. And then Allah limits the fighting and killing to a minimum, demanding that it stop as fast as possible and that there be no escalation in the kind of fighting.

Those jihads involving suicide bombing are especially troublesome to Allah. Even if the jihad would be just, assuming that Muslims were attacked first, suicide bombing would be a forbidden escalation unless the

161

Muslims were attacked by suicide bombers. And Allah has still other reasons to be against suicide.

## ALLAH DOES NOT LOOK KINDLY ON SUICIDE

Deliberately killing other Muslims under any circumstances is barred by the Koran, and is cursed by Allah (4.93), the uppermost expression of Allah's displeasure. Aside from the suicide bomber being a Muslim taking his or her own life, suicide bombings are indiscriminate and can take other Muslim lives as well. And although you might not like to accept it, the Koran treats Jews and Christians as believers who lives should not be taken:

*A believer should not kill a believer unless it is by mistake (4.92).*

*Allah curses, and punishes with hell, whoever intentionally kills a believer (4.93).*

*Whoever believes in God and the Last Day and does good, whether he be Muslim, Jew, Christian or Sabian, shall have their reward and should have no fear nor grieve on judgment day (2.62).*

The suicide bomber also offends Allah's life cycle plan. Allah created you and decreed your life-span. Your death is to come on you unawares and only Allah should know when it will happen. Death does not come unawares to a suicide bomber, obviously in violation of Allah's plan:

*Allah created you from clay and then decreed a fixed*

*lifespan for you (6.2).*
*Knowledge of your fixed time of death is only with Allah,*
*and death shall come on you unawares (7.187).*

The Koran also indicates that Muslims should not take their own lives:

*Do not cast yourself into perdition (2.195).*
*Do not kill yourselves (4.29).*

## EVERYONE MUST AWAIT THE DAY OF JUDGMENT BEFORE GOING TO PARADISE

There is no early way of getting into Paradise. Everybody must await the day of judgment, the day they will be resurrected and judged by Allah. The Koran provides that everybody must sleep in their graves and await the blowing of the trumpets. The heavens will burst asunder and the earth become empty before you are resurrected and brought before Allah for judgment and assignment to Paradise or Hell:

*Every person will receive their reward only on the day of*
*judgment (3.185).*
*Allah created man, made the way easy for him, caused*
*him to die, assigned a grave to him, and then, when*
*Allah wills it, He raises him to life again (80.19-22).*
*When the trumpet is sounded, the dead will rise from their*
*graves and hasten unto Allah (36.51).*
*When heaven bursts asunder and earth casts forth what is*
*in it, those who strove hard for Allah will be joyful*
*and the others will go into the burning fires of*

*perdition (84.1-12).*
**On the day when the earth crumbles to pieces and Allah comes with angels, hell will be made to appear and man will remember his record (89.21-23).**

The Koran is clear that everybody must await Allah calling the day of reckoning before anyone gets to go to Heaven.    They must await the divine call, a call accompanied by cataclysmic events that would be hard to ignore.  Only then will Paradise be opened to anyone.

If you think there is an exception for jihadists, you are mistaken.  Allah acknowledges that fighting in His cause is a ticket to Paradise, but the ticket has no date.  You cannot assume that an exception exists for jihads as there is nothing in the Koran to indicate an exception and much that shows that there is no exception.

Look carefully, Allah never says when the doors of Paradise will open for a person who fights in the way of Allah.  Nor is there any suggestion in the Koran that the slain will go to Paradise immediately while the victorious will have to await normal death:

**Whoever fights in the way of Allah, be he slain or be he victorious, shall be given a mighty reward by Allah (4.74).**

The Koran identifies those who have every expectation of a reward on the day of judgment, but in no case is it stated when that will take place:

164

*Those who have every expectation of a reward include those who:*

> *believe in God and the Last Day and do good (2.62).*
> *suffered exile and strove hard in the way of Allah (2.218).*
> *were driven from their homes, fought in Allah's way and were slain (3.195).*
> *do their duty to Allah (3.198).*
> *believe and do righteousness deeds (4.57).*
> *fights in the way of Allah, be he slain or be he victorious (4.74).*
> *believe and strive with their wealth and lives in the way of Allah (61.11-12).*

Allah's pattern should, by now, be clear to you. Assuming the cause is just, jihadists get a ticket to Paradise as does others who please Allah in other ways. And Allah provides no special treatment for any of the favored. All have to await the blowing of the trumpet and the cataclysmic events before Allah will open the doors of Paradise to any of them. It could happen tomorrow but you have to realize that the trumpets haven't yet blown and about 14 centuries have already passed since Allah started to reveal the Koran to Muhammad. Everybody still waits.

## DON'T CLING TO LIFE, BUT STILL YOU WON'T GET INTO PARADISE ANY FASTER

Allah extols Paradise and paints a wondrous picture of it. Life on earth is not to be clung to as Paradise is better for believers. It is not that Allah wants believers to give up their lives on earth so that they might go to the Hereafter, because Allah neither provides incentives to do so nor accelerates the time of entering Paradise. Allah's purpose in extolling Paradise is to get His believers to go forth in His way, to join the righteous fray and not shirk their duty or ask for exemptions:

*Life on earth is play and sport, with the Hereafter being a better abode for believers (6.32).*

*Life in this world is only an enjoyment, and the Hereafter is the abode to settle in (40.39).*

*Do not cling to life on earth which is little compared to the Hereafter (9.38).*

*Do not flee from unbelievers marching against you in war (8.15).*

*Believer should not ask for an exemption from fighting with their wealth and persons (9.44).*

## DO NOT BELIEVE THAT SEX AWAITS YOU IN PARADISE

Video testimonials made by prospective suicide bombers for their families indicate that they expect immediate admission to Paradise and wedding the black-eyed virgins there. This cannot be so on both accounts; there is no immediate admission nor is there sex in Paradise.

These soon-to-be suicide bombers will be sorely

disappointed as they will have to wait in their resting places until the judgment day call comes. You might not realize that this means that the suicide bomber might have had sex sooner had he lived out his life on earth and married in due course, as compared to waiting in the grave untold centuries for the trumpets to blow.

With all its references to beautiful companions, virgins and the like, the Koran never directly states that there is sex in Paradise. The Koran clearly and specifically says eat and drink, recline in bliss and observe beauty, but never says have sex. It never says that marriage can take place in Paradise. This is a sore omission for the Koran that speaks with distinctness as to sexual matters. There is much evidence to show that there is no sex in Paradise.

Marriage can not take place in Paradise. Allah has confirmed that He revealed the Christian Gospel and still guards it (3.3, 5.48, 10.37). The Koran had not abrogated what it said on this because there is nothing in the Koran to the contrary (2.106). Jesus said in the Gospel of Matthew[6] that there is no marriage and no sex in heaven and that has to also apply to Paradise. Perhaps the most telling point is that it is most difficult to claim that promiscuity is possible in Paradise when it is not to be otherwise found in the Koran and Islam is so conservative on matters relating to

---

[6] *"For in the resurrection they neither marry, nor are given in marriage, but are like angels in heaven."* *Matthew 22.30.* There is no sex amongst angels.

sex. Allah frowns on all forms of promiscuity, including adultery and fornication:

*Do not go near fornication as it is an obscenity (17.32).*

Sex in Paradise is only one of the false promises made to jihadists that have no underpinnings in the Koran. In addition to immediately available sex, the suicide bomber is told that he can take his family members to Paradise along with him. Some are told that they can select 70 people to take along with them to Paradise or designate them for future admission to Paradise. The Koran is to the contrary:

*On judgment day, the command judgment shall be entirely Allah's, and no person shall have power to do anything for another person (82.19).*

*On the day of judgment, every person will be paid in full what that person had earned (3.25).*

*Do not associate with Allah that for which He has given you no authority in His revelations (7.33).*

## LIFE IN PARADISE IS A PARABLE, NOT LITERAL

The Koran makes very clear that the descriptions of Paradise are only parables, meaning that they are not to be taken literally. Muhammad had been quoted as saying that the things of Paradise are not the things of this world; that nobody has seen, heard or conceived of them. It is all metaphorical as Allah confirms that man cannot know what is hidden in Paradise:

*No person knows what delights await in Paradise (32.17).*
*This is a parable of Paradise as promised to those who*
*    keep their duty:    therein rivers flow, fruits are*
*    perpetual and plenty, and there is shade (13.35).*
*This is a parable of Paradise promised to the dutiful:*
*    therein are rivers of water incorruptible, rivers of*
*    milk of unchanging taste; rivers of wine delicious to*
*    drinkers, and rivers of honey pure and clear (47.15).*

Thus, neither the rivers of Paradise nor anything else
said about Paradise in the Koran is meant to be taken
literally, as nobody can know or conceive of what is there.
Allah has kept Paradise hidden, telling everyone that He
has done so by calling what He had placed in the Koran a
parable.   As a result, Allah did not say what actually
existed in Paradise and says that readers should not take the
words literally.   Moreover, Allah says that nobody can or
should claim knowledge of what is in Paradise:

*The Koran consists of two types of verses.   There are the*
*    basic verses of substance that have clear and*
*    established meaning.    The others are allegorical*
*    verses the meanings of which are known only to*
*    Allah and cannot be known by man, and yet man*
*    causes discord by seeking to explain them (3.7).*
*[D]o not say about Allah that which you cannot know*
*    (7.33).*

The goodly and pure beauties in Paradise are not
actually to be found there for they are only a parable.
Whatever the blessings of Paradise are, and whatever exists
there, they are not of this world.   We are told so in the

Koran and also told so by Muhammad, and you should not accept anything to the contrary. If anything, this suggests that sex would not exist on Paradise as it is of this world.

The life in Paradise might well be a spiritual life and not of the physical kind we are familiar with on earth. All you can count on about Paradise is being closer to Allah spiritually. Those youthful suicide bombers seeking sex are much more likely to find it on earth.

## A FIGHTING JIHAD CANNOT BE AN INDIVIDUAL DUTY

When it comes to fighting, the Koran states that Muslims should act as a group, as a community, and not individually. The theme of unity and consensus appears in many Koranic verses. There is also a duty to bring peace to quarreling Muslims, or join to fight the wrongdoer. It is only in the case a personal jihad (that is, self-improvement jihads) where the person may act by himself or herself, which is the way it has to be in personal matters. But when it comes to fighting, the Koran wants a consensus so that the community fights all together:

*Fight all together as they fight you all together; but know that Allah is with those who restrain themselves (9.36).*

*Keep your bond to Allah and be all together, not disunited (3.103).*

So do not accept that you can have an individual duty to go out and kill people. The Koran shows that you have no individual duty to act against others. To be sure, you have an individual duty to yourself to pursue your individual self-improvement duty. But when it comes to acting against others, the Koran insists that the whole community be behind it, that there be consensus.


## DON'T GAMBLE ON PARADISE

Why a believing Muslim should deliberately destroy his or her chances of getting into Paradise is beyond understanding. The Koran shows with certainty the ways to achieve admission to Paradise, largely revolving around believing in Allah, adhering to the pillars of Islam, and doing things that are clearly good.

You will be responsible if you join an unjust jihad, and that is exactly what others are trying to foist on you. The promises made to you do not accord with the Koran and you should study the Koran if you are not already convinced.

# KORANIC VERSES

# Just & Unjust Jihads

Aside from a personal jihad to improve oneself, only defensive jihads against hostile attacks are in the way of Allah. No justification can be found for the innovative rhetoric of jihadists deeming attacks to exist where they do not. In this fashion, jihadists without Koranic justification start wars that make it seem like a clash of civilizations.

Yet, the wars do not speak of perpetual war for they are temporal, of this time. The underlying causes are transitory and will pass in time. Only the Koran is eternal and there is no prescription in the Koran for perpetual war between civilizations, as some would make it out to be.

An analysis of some ancient and some recent wars in terms of whether they could be considered justifiable jihads under the Koran would help in understanding the concept of a fighting jihad, which has to be defensive as demanded by the Koran:

*Fight in the way of Allah those who fight against you, but do not begin the hostilities (2.190).*

While exploring the just or unjust nature of the more recent jihads, the role of the United States is reviewed. The United States is not a Muslim nation but an attempt was made to apply Koranic standards to the discussion to see how the United Stated would fare in such an analysis. The result depends on how one looks at things, but the analysis does show that the United States was not being anti-Islam in doing what it did.

## THE ANCIENT WARS

The wars with Mecca were the first jihad. It was a just jihad because Muhammad was driven out of his home in Mecca in fear of his life and was later pursued by Meccan armies with weapons in their hands. All that transpired with the Meccans, who began the hostilities, should be considered as being in self-defense.

Some say that the subsequent Meccan attacks were in retaliation to Muslim attacks on Meccan caravans, as pillaging caravans was the only way the Muslims could then support themselves. But still, it could all be traced back to Muhammad having been driven from his home in what turned out to the *hijra*, the pilgrimage to Medina. The only possible issue I could detect is whether attacking the caravans presented an escalation of hostilities.

There is no question that there were some justifiable jihads amongst the other ancient battles.  For instance, the Mongols and the Turks attacked Islam (at different times) and the Muslims fought defensive wars against them.  Although the Muslims lost, those wars were in self-defense and properly considered just jihads.

The other wars of Islam, mostly the wars that so greatly expanded Islam, were a mixed bag.  The wars against the Roman Empire in Byzantine days and later against the Crusaders were defensive wars and should be considered justifiable jihads.

The very early wars within Arabia and many of those that followed were expansionary wars, not defensive wars, and cannot be considered just jihads.  Whether they were also wars to expand the religion, which they must have been in part for at least some Muslims, would be irrelevant since they would still be unjust jihads not in the way of Allah since Allah forbids the use of compulsion in religion (2.256).

But those were not wars to convert people to Islam. The very early Arabian wars, before the fighting Bedouins became Muslims, were wars for spoils and booty from their viewpoint.  The conversion of conquered Arabs to Islam was no more than an insignificant rationale for the fighting

Muslims who were then mostly interested in subduing and civilizing the land they lived in, not using force in religion.

Initially, when the Arab Muslims began to attack areas outside of Arabia, the Muslims did not want conversions. In those days, it was felt that Islam was an Arab religion. The Muslim victors merely placed troops in newly constructed garrison towns, leaving the conquered people to go about their business as *dhimmi*. As the Muslims weren't being attacked first, it is difficult to make the case that the initial expansion of Islam was based on just jihads even though the soon to be compiled Koran forbad wars not in self-defense.

## RECENT WARS

The recent wars in the Middle East involved the United States and, for the most part, can be considered just jihads with the United States being on the right side of those jihads.

**Afghanistan.** The first jihad arose in response to the 1979 Russian invasion of Afghanistan. The Russian attack was not in response to any attack on Russia by Afghan Muslims or by the Afghan state. The Afghan Muslims were clearly fighting in self-defense in trying to stop the Russians who attacked for their own political reasons. Other Muslims joined to help the Afghan defense, including both Osama bin Laden and the United States, the latter clandestinely but extensively through its secret intelligence agency, the C.I.A.

Although the Americans helped the Afghan Muslims for political and not religious reasons based on the Koran, the United States did in fact go to the aid of Muslims, Afghan Muslims, and America helped substantially in causing the Russians to withdraw in 1989. Thus, the United States participated on the right side in a just Muslim jihad.

The Muslim victory against the superpower Russians may arguably be attributable more to the supply of modern arms, intelligence and advice by the Americans than to the outstandingly brave and extraordinarily fierce Afghan Muslims. However, victory did belong to the Afghans. The Russian withdrawal allowed Muslims everywhere to judge that Islam defeated a superpower, and that later allowed Osama bin Laden to claim top honors. The just jihad reclaimed status and prestige for Islam and also provided exaggerated bragging rights for participating extremists like bin-Laden.

The Afghan war turned out to initiate a new pattern where Islam generally ignored those instances where America was on the right side of just Muslim jihads. America is supposed to be the target, according to the jihadists, and their extremist *ulama* cannot allow Muslim society to acknowledge that America had helped on the right side of a just Muslim jihad. Thus, they rewrite history as extremists everywhere have been known to do.

**Kosovo and Bosnia.** About 80% of the ethnic Albanians living in Yugoslavian Kosovo were Muslim. They were being persecuted and killed by Yugoslavian Christian Serbs, as they had been for centuries, but it started to look like an active genocide in 1999. The United States joined in the defensive of the Muslims and quickly committed much air power to an allied endeavor, which was successful in stopping the killing of the Muslims in a few months.

Previously, the Muslim population in nearby Bosnia-Herzegovina was under attack and siege for years, also by the Yugoslavian Christian Serbs and Coats, until finally in 1995 the United States acted to bring about a settlement negotiated in the American city of Dayton, in the State of Ohio. United States involvement came late but was effective in stopping the massacre of Bosnian Muslims, unfortunately after some 200,000 were killed. Next time around, in Kosovo, America acted with much more speed.

In both Kosovo and Bosnia, it is likely that most or all of the Muslim populations would have been wiped out but for United States intervention. The Muslims were fighting in defense in a just jihad that the United States joined solely for humanitarian purposes as it had no economic or political interests of its own, as it did in stopping the Russians in Afghanistan.

Those were sterling acts on the part of the United States on behalf of Muslims in both Kosovo and Bosnia, with no self-interest involved, but it did not get the credit it deserved in Islam for some unexplained reasons. Rather, ordinary Muslims seemed to accept the anti-United States rhetoric of the extremist *ulama* that continued to make it an enemy and a target, ignoring the reality that the United States' actions showed it was not anti-Islamic.

**Saddam Hussein War #1.**  The three wars fought by Saddam Hussein, dictator of Iraq, are being called Saddam Hussein Wars I, II and III because it is difficult to say that the people of Iraq conducted the wars. To taint Iraq or the Iraqi people with those wars would be unfair, as Hussein clearly did not represent most of the Iraqi people. Saddam Hussein attacked other nations but also brutally attacked and repressed his own people.

Saddam Hussein War # I was against Iran, Muslim state against Muslim state. These states had been fighting, off and on for a while. Muslims are not supposed to fight other Muslims. Such a war cannot be in the cause of Allah, and thus it cannot be a jihad:

*All believers are brethren and you have a duty to make peace between your contending brethren (49.10).*
*A believer should not kill a believer unless it is by mistake*

*(4.92).*
*Allah curses, and punishes with hell, whoever intentionally kills a believer (4.93).*

In this war, which ended in 1988, the United States could be considered on the side of Saddam Hussein because it supplied him with weapons. Yet, a jihad was not involved. Although the United States was clearly on the wrong side on a moral basis, it cannot be said to have participated on the wrong side of a jihad.

The United States must have had some economic or political purpose in mind, which purpose is not presently apparent in history, but it could not be considered anti-Islam because both states were Muslim. The United States owes an apology to Iran for this even though it was not acting anti-Muslim.

**Saddam Hussein War #2.** In War #2, Saddam Hussein blatantly attacked Kuwait in 1990, again pitting Muslim state against Muslim state. In defense, Kuwait asked for assistance and other Muslim states and the United States came to its aid.

The Koran addresses situations like this. Allah instructs Muslims to make peace between quarreling Muslims and failing that, join to fight the wrongdoer. Saddam Hussein was the aggressor and wrongdoer, with there being no way to settle the quarrel as Hussein had already attacked Kuwait. A number of Muslim states went to the aid of Kuwait. Joining to fight the wrongdoer is in the way of Allah, and thus be the subject of a just jihad, as that is what Allah instructs:

*If parties of believers quarrel, make peace between them with fairness and justice. If one party does wrong to the other, fight the one who does wrong until they obey Allah (49.9).*

Thus, once again the United States was on the right side, whether or not that war viewed as a typical jihad. Saddam Hussein's armies were driven out of Kuwait, and the county was freed. Unfortunately, it was decided not to bring the battle into Iraq, which could be done in pursuing a just jihad, and Saddam Hussein remained around to start War #3.

**Saddam Hussein War #3.**  Saddam Hussein would be the aggressor in War #3 if War #3 is viewed as a continuation of War #2, which is a most reasonable interpretation of events even though War #3 started in 2003, thirteen years later. This view is based on War #2 not being finished. War #2 represented a just war or just defensive jihad against an aggressor with the United States being on the right side, and that would also apply to War #3 as the continuation. If War #3 is not considered to be a continuation of War #2, a separate evaluation is required.

United Nations resolutions condemned Saddam

Hussein for violation of his agreements that ended War #2. Enforcement of those resolutions by invading Iraq was threatened by the United Nations in a number of resolutions over the years. More than a decade passed and Iraq was finally invaded so as to enforce the United Nations resolution, but it is unclear whether the United Nations or the United States actually pressed the invasion button.

The United States claims that the United Nations had done enough to authorize the enforcement invasion even though the United Nations never passed a resolution to that exact effect. The United States claimed that it was enforcing a whole string of United Nations resolutions in response to Saddam Hussein's numerous breaches. Others ascribe less honorable reasons to the United States attacking Iraq, some of them being nefarious reasons.

So it becomes a mixed bag, with the United States being clearly on the right side in War #2, and the wrong side on War #1 (although that could not be a jihad since it was Muslim against Muslim), and in never-never land in War #3. War #3 depends on how you look at it.

There are a number of things that could be said about War #3 even though at the time of this writing, Iraq is still unsettled and the United States forces are still on the receiving end of bombs being thrown by jihadists and some others. Before the United States involvement, the major segment of the Iraqi population, the Shiite Muslims with

60% of the population, were being persecuted and killed, and were totally disenfranchised. It is clear that the United States stopped the persecution and killings and now the Shiite not only have a franchise but are in majority control of their own nation because of the United States involvement -- score that for being on the right side, although some Sunni might not feel that way.

Before the United States involvement, the Sunni Muslims who were not of Saddam Hussein's particular Sunni clan were also oppressed, killed and tortured, but not nearly to the extent of the Shiite Muslims. Most of the Sunni had also effectively lost their franchise to the dictator. This too was reversed by the United States involvement -- also score this for being the right side. America also helped free the Kurdish population in Iraq and get them a franchise -- another score on the right side.

On the other side of the ledger, United States troops were killing Muslims in defending themselves against bombings and other attacks. While United States would say that its troops were there in aid of Iraqi Muslims and thus on the right side, the jihadists would say that it was an aggressive act on the part of United State and not in aid of Muslims. The jihadists would argue that they were conducting a defensive jihad against a United States attack -- if not a United States attack against Iraq, then against the Islamic religion.

The United States response would be that hadn't attacked the Iraqi people nor the Islamic religion, and the religion was never endangered;  that it attacked only Saddam Hussein and his henchman pursuant to United Nations authority and all the other groups involved themselves for political advantage.  And so it goes.  War #3 is very complex in terms of jihad evaluation.

## THE JUST UNITED STATES "JIHAD" AGAINST
## AL QAEDA AND THE TALIBAN

On all scores, the September 11, 2001 suicide attacks on the United States must be considered to be an unjustifiable jihad by the Al Qaeda organization, making it criminal murders.  There were many distinct violations of Koranic dictates.

1).  Al Qaeda arguments of deemed attacks by America are specious.  There was nothing defensive about the Al Qaeda attacks.  Muslims are allowed to attack only when they are attacked first, and Al Qaeda attacked the United States first.

2).  The September 11 attacks were not of like-kind to anything that went before.  Muslims are allowed only to retaliate in kind, while the use of suicide attacks would constitute a clear escalation to any deemed attack by the United States.

3).  Al Qaeda was acting independently of any community consensus. The Koran insists that Muslims act all together, necessitating consensus and state action.  The consensus of Muslims was that the September 11 attacks were unjustified and no Muslim state backed it.

4).  The September 11 attacks were conducted by suicides, which the Koran shuns, and which offends Allah's plans for life and death.

5).  The September 11 attacks knowingly and deliberately killed Muslims, in direct violation of the dictates of the Koran.  It was know that Muslims would be killed in the massive attacks, and it could not be considered unintentional.

Al Qaeda had been an indirect ally of the United States in the war against the Russians in Afghanistan that ended in 1989, at which time Al Qaeda effectively started.  Al Qaeda played no role in the Saddam Hussein War # 2 against Kuwait in 1990, where the United States came to the aid of that Muslin nation and was on the right side of a jihad.  At the time Al Qaeda attacked the United States in 2001, two years before Saddam Hussein War #3, Al Qaeda could claim no United States attack on Muslims anywhere -- to the contrary, the United States had only gone to the aid of Muslims.  The deemed attacks Al Qaeda dredged up in its attempt to justify its attack on the United States were specious.

The United States has no state religion, but if Koranic principles were applied, the United States response to the September 11 attacks would be a justifiable jihad.  The

United States was attacked first (22.39, 60.8). The United States response of seeking out the attackers and attacking them where they were to be found (in Taliban Afghanistan), was a proper response (2.191). The response was of like-kind (2.194, 16.126), taking life and limb for life and limb, less heinous than the forbidden suicide bombings (2.195, 4.29, 7.187). The people of the United States duly reached a consensus in its legislature to fight back, acting all together (3.103, 9.36). Al Qaeda was found in the country of Afghanistan, where its headquarters and training bases were located:

Because it harbored Al Qaeda's headquarters and training bases, Afghanistan might also be viewed as an indirect participant in the September 11 attacks on the United States. Before retaliating, the United States had asked the Taliban government of Afghanistan to turn over the Al Qaeda people harbored there but the Taliban refused to do so. The United States response conducted on Afghanistan soil was justified under Koranic standards.

Thus, in recent years, the United States fought on the right side of Islam jihads on 4 occasions; in Afghanistan against the Russians, in Kosovo, in Bosnia, and in Saddam Hussein War #2. Also, applying Koranic standards to the September 11 attacks, the United States would be on the right side on a 5<sup>th</sup> occasion: in Afghanistan against Al Qaeda). The terrorists and extremist *ulama* have no grounds to accuse the United States of being anti-Islam.

# Responding to the Ayatollah Khomeini, Osama Bin-Laden & Hizbullah

To enable you to settle any doubts you may have as to whether the extremist *ulama* and terrorists misrepresent the Koran, I compare the writings of the Ayatollah Khomeini, Osama Bin-Laden and Hizbullah with the plain language of the Koran. The Ayatollah's furious 1984 speech is used, as is bin-Laden's World Islamic Front statement entitled *"Jihad Against Jews and Crusaders."* Hizbullah's rationale was found in the book *"Hizbu'llah, Politics and Religion*[7]*"* and used for this purpose although the book was not written by Hizbullah, but Hizbullah purportedly did review it.

Representing a broad depiction of extremist rhetoric,

---

[7] Amal Saad-Ghorayeb, Pluto Press, London, 2002.

these writings are analyzed in terms of the Koran, the sole focus of this book. References to non-Koranic sources is not discussed as it is felt that they cannot stand-up if in conflict with the Koran and are not needed if in agreement with the Koran.

The rhetoric in these extremist statements consists of both exhortations to the faithful to do the writers' bidding, and justifications of the positions that the writers had adopted. All three contain diatribes against the targeted culprits, usually the West or the State of Israel. As the leader of the West, the United States is frequently the focus of criticism. The term "Crusaders" is used by the extremists as a proxy for the United States as it is considered a Christian country and the association with the Crusaders is aimed at being derogatory in Islam.

# Ayatollah Khomeini's Fierce Rhetoric

The Ayatollah Khomeini rhetoric is an exhortation to his followers to wage war and kill, stated in terms that seem particularly hateful. Khomeini had reason to hate as his son was killed, and his "Great Satan" (the United States) did do something that it should apologize for, namely, the United States help Saddam Hussein in war against Iran

(Saddam Hussein War #1). Nevertheless, as you will learn, what the Ayatollah said did not square with the Koran -- and hopefully represents a personal attitude that is not adopted by his successors. The Ayatollah died in 1989.

The selected statement by the Ayatollah Ruhollah Khomeini (1902?-1989) is an excerpt taken from a speech he gave in 1984, some five years after he was successful in leading a revolution in Iran disposing of the prior secular Pahlavi government and establishing an Islamic state with some democratic attributes. At that time, it might be said that the United States did not really understand Islam, particularly not the Shiite in Iran, and the United States talked itself into demonizing Iran into an enemy.

Iraq under Saddam Hussein had attacked Iran in 1980, a war that was to go on for some eight years and end in a standoff after killing over a half million people. Iraq was backed by the Saudis, who are Sunni and the traditional rivals of the Shiite in Iran. Iraq and Saudi Arabia are Arab, while Iran is not Arab but largely Persian in heritage. The Shiite holy places are in Iraq, but the Shiite population is greater in Iran. The Shiite in Iraq were being severely repressed by Saddam Hussein.

The United States extended help directly to the likes of Saddam Hussein, the tyrant dictator of Iraq. It is odd indeed how a distorted, amoral[8] view of the "national interest" can make for such strange bedfellows. The hateful remarks of the Ayatollah should be understood in this historic context. This is what the Ayatollah Khomeini said in his 1984 speech:

> If infidels are allowed to continue playing their role of corrupters on Earth, their eventual moral punishment will be all the stronger. Thus, if we kill the infidels to put a stop to their corrupting activities, we have indeed done them a service, because their eventual punishment will be less. To allow the infidels to stay alive means to let them do more corrupting. Killing them is a surgical operation commanded by Allah the Creator. Those who follow the Koran are aware that we have to kill. War is a blessing for the world and for every nation. It is Allah himself who commands men to wage war and to kill.

---

[8] *The Necessary Amorality of Foreign Affairs*, by Arthur Schlesinger, Jr., Harper's, August 1971. This article was reprinted in *An American Album, One Hundred and Fifty Years of Harper's Magazine*, Lewis H. Lapham, Editor, LPC Group, New York, April 1, 2000 -- innocuous alterations were made in the article, but the title was meaningfully changed in 2000 to *Is There a Place for Morality in Foreign Affairs?* and the date retained as August 1971. It would seem that the change in title essentially reflected the increasing morality in the determination of the national interest in the United States during the interim, a change that continues to this day.

**Fault #1:**     The term "infidel" is the classically pejorative *ulama* word for a person who does not believe in Islam.  Pagans, idolaters, and polytheists are other terms for unbelievers.

The Koran specifically states that unbelievers are to be treated fairly and tolerantly.  Yet, the Ayatollah tarnishes them with an accusation not to be found in the Koran, and does not show the kindness, justice or forgiveness the Koran demands:

*Allah requires that you respect, show kindness and deal justly with those who do not fight with you for religion or drive you from your homes (60.8).*
*Believers should forgive those who do not believe (45.14).*

**Fault #2:**   Nor does the Koran allow any people to be viewed and condemned as a group.  The Koran requires that people be viewed independently.  Yet the Ayatollah condemns all "infidels" as a group:

*People of a group are not all alike (3.113).*
*There are good people amongst the Jews who speak the truth and do justice with it (7.159).*

**Fault #3:**    The Ayatollah declares what the spiritual punishment of Allah will be on judgment day, which he cannot possibly know.   The Ayatollah says that the eventual punishment of the infidels, by Allah, will be greater.   The claim of such knowledge goes against the Koran:

*[D]o not say about Allah that which you cannot know*

*(7.33).*

**Fault #4:** The Ayatollah obviously targets Jews and the Christian West as they are not Muslims, which is what infidel means. Yet, Jews and Christians are treated throughout the Koran as believers, and the Koran incorporates the Scriptures of the Jews and the Christians:

*Allah has revealed the Koran to you, and verifies that He also revealed the Torah and Gospel (3.3).*

*Whoever believes in God and the Last Day and does good, whether he be Muslim, Jew, Christian or Sabian, shall have their reward and should have no fear nor grieve on judgment day (2.62).*

*Allah curses, and punishes with hell, whoever intentionally kills a believer (4.93).*

Thus, Jews and Christians are believers entitled to be considered for admission to Paradise and sit alongside Muslims, based on individual judgment:

*In a promise binding on Allah in the Torah, Gospel and Koran, Allah admits to Paradise believers who devote their persons and their property fighting in God's way (9.111).*

**Fault #5:** Allah has not labeled any group, and certainly not the Jews and Christians, as corrupters. If anything, Allah is partial to the Jews and Christians, treating them as believers, allowing Muslims to marry them (the Prophet Muhammad's 10th wife, Safiyya, was Jewish) and eat Jewish food. Allah had even protected Jewish and Christian houses of worship:

*It is lawful for Muslims to eat the food of Jews[9] and Christians and marry their chaste women (5.5).*

*But for Allah's protection, monasteries, churches, synagogues and mosques where God's name is often mentioned would have been torn down (22.40).*

**Fault #6:**  The Ayatollah proposes early killing of non-Muslims (infidels) so as to reduce Allah's eventual penalty, but, even there, he is assuming a godlike knowledge or awareness of what will be on judgment day. For all he knows, the infidels, if left alive, could stop their "corrupting" and start doing good or become Muslims. Even apostates, so disliked in Islam, can repent and return to Allah.  Thus, the Ayatollah would be eliminating any chance of change, repentance or adoption of Islam, which goes against the Koran and is not in the way of Allah:

*Non-believers who repent, changing their ways and holding fast to Allah, will be accepted as believers (4.146).*

**Fault # 7:**  "Surgical" killing or not (whatever that means), Allah does not allow the Ayatollah or his followers to kill infidels or kill the corrupt under the circumstances the Ayatollah advances.  The Ayatollah is claiming that Muslims have the right or duty to kill infidels merely because they are infidels and kill the corrupt merely because they are corrupt, just as extremist *ulama* have

---

[9]  According to the Koran (6.121), animals must be slaughtered while mentioning the name of God, and Jews do this in their slaughter ritual.

made the same claims over the centuries. Yet the fact remains that Allah, in the eternal Koran, only gives Muslims permission to kill when they are attacked first:

*Allah permits Muslins to fight if war is first made on them (22.39).*

*Fight in the way of Allah against those who fight against you, but do not begin the hostilities. Allah does not love aggressors (2.190).*

**Fault # 8:** To say that Allah commands Muslims to wage war and kill shows the Ayatollah to be a master at rhetoric. It sounds as if Allah issued a standing order for Muslims to go out and kill, which couldn't be further from what the Koran says. Allah gave only limited, very limited permission for Muslims to kill, and that permission was situation specific; the Muslims had to have been attacked first. There was no blanket approval in advance to go out and kill although the Ayatollah makes it look that way.

The Ayatollah starts with the Koranic verse that command Muslims to fight even though they personally dislike fighting and he ignores the limitations the Koran places on fighting. What the Koran is saying that Muslims have to fight when the duty falls on them to fight, as when they are attacked first. It is not a declaration that Muslims should be warlike and just go out and fight and kill at will, as some extremist *ulama* would have it.

With life having been made sacred, some believers would naturally be reluctant to take sacred lives, while others might merely be shirkers. The Koranic verse acknowledges that Muslims would naturally dislike taking sacred lives:

*You should not take life made sacred by Allah, except by way of Allah's law and justice (6.151).*
*Fighting is prescribed for you though it may be hateful to you (2.216).*
*Do not flee before unbelievers marching against you in war (8.15).*

**Fault #9:**    Nothing can be found in the Koran to support the Ayatollah's contention that war is a blessing for the world and for every nation. There is no telling where this comes from. Islam is a religion of peace even though the Ayatollah's contention would make it into a religion of war. War has been the path of the extremist *ulama* since antiquity, not the path of Allah.

While the Ayatollah's statement is criticized here, and some commentators call it mad or worse, it should be understood that the Ayatollah had reason to be angry. His son had been killed and his nation gassed by Saddam Hussein, disgracefully helped by the United States. It is no wonder why the United State became the "Great Satan" to the Ayatollah and the Ayatollah resorted to tirades. Both owe apologies. But the fact of the matter remains that the Ayatollah misrepresented the Koran. The Koran does not say what he said and actually stands to the contrary.

# Osama Bin-Laden's
# Flawed Justifications

Osama bin-Laden (Usamah Bin-Muhammad Bin-Laden) is of the Saudi establishment. His father is influential and very wealthy. His father had four wives, a number of concubines and many children. Osama was the only child of his mother who was divorced by her husband, lowering her and Osama's status.

Osama bin-Laden was born in the secular capital of Saudi Arabia, Riyadh. He was successful in his own right as a construction company owner, which obviously taught him people and management skills. As a terrorist, he probably owes more to the Ayatollah Khomeini and the United States government than any upbringing, education or training he got in Saudi Arabia.

The Ayatollah's successful revolution energized those of an extremist mind like bin-Laden by showing that an Islamic revolution could be successful in the modern age. The factual situation in Iran was somewhat unusual. There were a number of opposition groups in Iran, in particular the communists, which were at the core of the Iranian revolution.

The Ayatollah ultimately won, it is said, by double

crossing the communists in the complicated game that was played in Iran. Perversely, that might have been in the United States interest lest the communist compatriots to the next-door Russians, hated at the time by the United States, took over in Iran. What the United States did behind the scene is not known. For all we know, the United States might have assisted against the communists. Russia was then a communist nation, perhaps assisting the Iranian communists.

The United States had helped bin-Laden by supplying the wherewithal for the Afghans to defeat the Russians. Arab extremists flocked to help the Afghans, including bin-Laden who was wounded a few times in the process. The United States withdrew abruptly after the Russians left, not knowing Islam and the ramifications of leaving nor even discussing it internally. Bin-Laden claimed bragging rights as the victor and his reputation swelled. From fledging operations of good assistance to the Afghan fighters, Al Qaeda became the Afghanistan powerbroker; delivered to bin-Laden by none other than the United States.

Al Qaeda broadened its opposition to the United States, first, because of the existence of a U.S. military airbase on sacred Saudi territory (at the invitation of the Saudis) and, later, because of the mileage Al Qaeda got from criticizing the United States support of Israel. By this time Al Qaeda began to treat the United States as a paper tiger, directly attacking U.S. installations, attacking a U.S.

naval vessel and finally attacking in New York City and Washington DC on September 11, 2001.

The bin-Laden statement analyzed here was issued on February 23, 1998, three years before the September 11 attacks. The issue date was 8 years after Saddam Hussein's War against Kuwait and five years before the present fighting in Iraq began. Al Qaeda joined with four associated organizations, called the World Islamic Front, and labeled their statement *Jihad Against Jews and Crusaders*:

> Praise be to God, who revealed the Book, controls the clouds, defeats factionalism, and says in His Book: But when the forbidden months are past, then fight and slay the pagans wherever ye find them, seize them, beleaguer them, and lie in wait for them in every stratagem (of war); and peace be upon our Prophet, Muhammad Bin-'Abdallah, who said: I have been sent with the sword between my hands to ensure that no one but God is worshipped, God who put my livelihood under the shadow of my spear and who inflicts humiliation and scorn on those who disobey my orders.
>
> The Arabian Peninsula has never -- since God made it flat, created its desert, and encircled it with seas -- been stormed by any forces like the crusader armies spreading in it like locusts, eating its riches and wiping out its plantations. All this is happening at a time in which nations are attacking Muslims like people fighting over a plate of food. In the light of the grave situation and the lack of support, we and you are obliged to discuss current events, and we should all

agree on how to settle the matter.

No one argues today about three facts that are known to everyone; we will list them, in order to remind everyone:

First, for over seven years the United States has been occupying the lands of Islam in the holiest of places, the Arabian Peninsula, plundering its riches, dictating to its rulers, humiliating its people, terrorizing its neighbors, and turning its bases in the Peninsula into a spearhead through which to fight the neighboring Muslim peoples.

If some people have in the past argued about the fact of the occupation, all the people of the Peninsula have now acknowledged it. The best proof of this is the Americans' continuing aggression against the Iraqi people using the Peninsula as a staging post, even though all its rulers are against their territories being used to that end, but they are helpless.

Second, despite the great devastation inflicted on the Iraqi people by the crusader-Zionist alliance, and despite the huge number of those killed, which has exceeded 1 million... despite all this, the Americans are once against trying to repeat the horrific massacres, as though they are not content with the protracted blockade imposed after the ferocious war or the fragmentation and devastation.

So here they come to annihilate what is left of this people and to humiliate their Muslim neighbors.

Third, if the Americans' aims behind these wars are religious and economic, the aim is also to serve the Jews' petty state and divert attention from its occupation of Jerusalem and murder of Muslims there. The best proof of this is their eagerness to destroy Iraq, the strongest neighboring Arab state, and their endeavor to fragment all the states of the region such as Iraq, Saudi Arabia, Egypt, and Sudan into paper statelets and through their disunion and weakness to guarantee Israel's survival and the continuation of the brutal crusade occupation of the Peninsula.

All these crimes and sins committed by the Americans are a clear declaration of war on God, his messenger, and Muslims. And ulama have throughout Islamic history unanimously agreed that the jihad is an individual duty if the enemy destroys the Muslim countries. This was revealed by Imam Bin-Qadamah in 'Al-Mughni,' Imam Al-Kisa'i in 'Al-Bada'i,' al-Qurtubi in his interpretation, and the shaykh of al-Islam in his books, where he said: As for the fighting to repulse [an enemy], it is aimed at defending sanctity and religion, and it is a duty as agreed [by the ulama]. Nothing is more sacred than belief except repulsing an enemy who is attacking religion and life.

On that basis, and in compliance with God's order, we issue the following fatwa to all Muslims:

The ruling to kill the Americans and their allies -- civilians and military -- is an individual duty for every Muslim who can do it in any country in which it is possible to do it, in order to liberate the al-Aqsa Mosque and the holy mosque [Mecca] from their grip, and in order for their armies to move out of all the lands of Islam, defeated and unable to threaten any Muslim. This is in accordance with the words of Almighty God, and fight the pagans all together as they fight you all together, and fight them until there is no more tumult or oppression, and there prevail justice and faith in God.

This is in addition to the words of Almighty God: And why should ye not fight in the cause of God and of those who, being weak, are ill-treated (and oppressed)? -- women and children, whose cry is: Our Lord, rescue us from this town, whose people are oppressors; and raise for us from thee one who will help!

We -- with God's help -- call on every Muslim who believes in God and wishes to be rewarded to comply with God's order to kill the Americans and plunder their money wherever and whenever they find it. We also call on Muslim ulama, leaders, youths, and soldiers to launch the raid on Satan's United States troops and the devil's supporters allying with them, and to displace those who are behind them so that they may learn a lesson.

Almighty God said: O ye who believe, give your response to God and His Apostle, when He calleth you to that which will give you life. And know that God cometh between a man and his heart, and that it is He to whom ye shall all be gathered. Almighty God also says: O ye who believe, what is the matter with you, that when ye are asked to go forth in the cause of God, ye cling so heavily to the earth! Do ye prefer the life of this world to the hereafter? But little is the comfort of this life, as compared with the hereafter. Unless ye go forth, He will punish you with a grievous penalty, and put others in your place; but Him ye would not harm in the least. For God hath power over all things.

God also says: So lose no heart, nor fall into despair. For ye must gain mastery if ye are true in faith.

## LET US NOT BE CONFUSED BY THE FACTS

**Airbase:** The first and presumably major injustice advanced by bin-Laden is the U.S. airbase built in the sacred land of Saudi Arabia in reaction to Saddam Hussein's invasion of neighboring Kuwait (Saddam Hussein War #2). The airbase construction obviously had the approval of the House of Saud, if not built at their request. Somehow this was distorted into plundering the wealth of Saudi Arabia, dictating to its rulers, and causing humiliation, whereas in actual fact the Saudis controlled the use of the base and denied its use by the United States in the fighting in Iraq (Saddam Hussein War #3).

If bin-Laden's true and ultimate target is the House of Saud, as many commentators believe, bin-Laden probably viewed the airbase as a guarantor of the House of Saud and felt he had to get rid of it. As it turned out, the United States closed the air base shortly after the Saddam Hussein War #3 began for reasons that will probably remain buried for generations.[10]

Perhaps the closing was initiated by the United States in reaction to increasing criticism of the United States propping up governments (which would incidentally be supportive of bin-Laden's purpose) or in reaction to the Saudi's non-action after September 11th and with respect to

---

[10] *The Saudi Exit: No Sure Cure For Royals' Troubles*, By Patrick E. Tyler, The New York Times, April 30, 2003.

Saddam Hussein War #3. Perhaps the United States felt it had to respond to the Saudi rejection of the probable American requests to use the base in War #3.

Perhaps the airbase was closed to withdraw a level of security so that the House of Saud would pay more attention to reining in the extremists instead of relying on working things out. Perhaps it was to relocate the base to obtain more flexible use in the future. Perhaps it wasn't closed at the initiative of the United States at all, and the Saudi's demanded it (which is doubted since they did have effective control over its use). Nevertheless, the base closing denies bin-Laden's arguing point based on his incorrect concept of sacred land.

**Sacred land:** Apparently, bin-Laden believes that Saudi Arabian land is getting more sacred as the centuries pass. Or perhaps he says so, inaccurate as it is, as an appealing slogan to rally support and obtain recruits. Bin-Laden calls the entire Arabian Peninsula the "holiest of places." Perhaps it's just his pride of birth, or perhaps he is demeaning the rest of Islam, like the Shiite holy places in Iraq. The Koran confers no such honor to the Arabian Peninsula, Saudi Arabia, or even the Arabian Hijaz area where Mecca and Medina are located. The sacred territory is the city of Mecca plus a few miles of land around it where fighting is forbidden:

*Allah made the city of Mecca sacred (27.91).*
*Allah secured the sacred territory of Mecca from violence*

*(29.67).*

Certainly the Kaba is sacred and so is the rest of the ancient city of Mecca. It is not clear that the modern expanded metropolitan area, with its huge airport and advanced facilities, was covered in Koranic view of Mecca. Nor is the import of the word "sacred" clear. In many religions, non-believers can visit sacred sites. Allah made the Sacred Mosque open, but with limitations:

*Allah has made the Sacred Mosque open to all of mankind [who adopt Islam] (22.25).*
*Pagans, being unclean, are forbidden to come near the Sacred Mosque (9.28).*

As it is now, non-Muslims are barred from the entire Mecca area and not just from the Sacred Mosque. Bin-Laden comes along and would make all Saudi Arabia a sacred place, for which there is no authority in the Koran. The House of Saud can be said to concur, for if the airbase were on sacred soil, the House of Saud would not have allowed it to be built.

**Iraq:** Bin-Laden's second complaint is the great devastation allegedly inflicted on the people of Iraq by the Jews and Crusaders (meaning Christians, and hence meaning Americans). Not even bin-Laden would talk favorably about Saddam Hussein, the murderous Iraqi ruler, but he does attribute Saddam Hussein's horrific massacres to the Jews and Christians and also attribute to them the United Nations blockade. It appears as though

Bin-Laden would like to rewrite history but stops short of doing so.

**Israel:**    The third grievance is the "petty state" of Israel.    Bin-Laden was late in joining the political opposition to Israel, probably to avoid diluting his real focus on Saudi Arabia, but he did so eventually because it could get him recruits.    He ties his opposition into his expanded territorial concept of the Islamic "holy" land by calling Israel the brutal crusade occupation of the Arabian Peninsula.

Bin-Laden's obvious theme of protecting the homeland would be a populist refrain.    But neither the homeland nor Mecca is being threatened by either the Jews or modern "Crusaders."    If anything, the homeland is being used as an internal weapon within Islam, as some Muslims and Muslim states support putting Mecca under multi-national Muslim control and operation.

**Humiliation:**    Bin Laden uses humiliation, or more accurately attempts to create humiliation in his fellow Muslims as a means of inflaming them and thus eliciting support.    He goes on to suggest that the aim of the Jews and the American is to turn four nations, Iraq, Saudi Arabia, Egypt, and Sudan into "paper statelets," which would be more would-be humiliations.    There is no apparent pattern in this listing of Muslim nations, although the omission of Syria seems curious.

The true humiliation, if there is any at all, is in Muslim nations not being able to develop internally due to the repression and divisiveness of their own extremist *ulama* and having to devote time, energy and treasure to fend off terrorist organizations.

**Crusades:**   Bin-Laden's use of the word Crusader, instead of Christian, is of course a ploy to demonize the Christians of today by associating them with those who attacked Islam centuries ago.  Since fighting the Crusaders of old was a justifiable jihad against those who attacked first, bin-Laden tries to get legitimacy for his unjust jihads because he opposes the Crusader straw-man he set up.  Bin-Laden neglects to mention that there is no inherited sin in Islam, so what happened before is irrelevant:

*The ancient Jews and Christians have passed away and theirs is what they had earned, while their progeny earn what is theirs and are not to be asked what their ancestors did (2.141).*

Linking Jews and Crusaders makes it appear that the Jews were linked to the Crusader attacks on Islam, whereas in historic fact the Jews fought alongside Muslims to repel the Crusaders; and the Crusaders slaughtered Jews and Muslims alike without discrimination.

**America:**   Bin-Laden claims that America's aims "behind these wars are religious, economic and political," pretty much coving the entire landscape.  Of course, bin-Laden and his friends have no agenda other than stopping

206

America. All political actives, including bin-Laden, have their own aims and that itself should not be a criticism. The criticism would be in exactly what those aims are, for America as well as bin-Laden.

Bin-Laden criticizes American aims, avoiding mention of what they are, nor does he say what his aims are. Many believe bin-Laden's real purpose is to unseat the House of Saud, something he would not talk about. Naturally, he doesn't mention that the United States went to the aid of Muslims a number of times (for example, in Kosovo and Bosnia) where it had no religious, economic or political aims, but only humanitarian aims.

**Factionalism:** Knowing the Koran, bin-Laden and his friends pay lip service to consensus and unity because of the especially important role non-divisiveness plays in the Koran. Right at the beginning bin-Laden refers to the defeat of factionalism, a true Islamic purpose, but one most violated by him. Bin Laden and his friends cannot gain legitimacy as they have no consensus behind them.

Bin-Laden does not stand for solidarity and consensus as he has the support of no nation. He and Al Qaeda operate without community consensus, and in opposition to it. By deliberately giving lip service to the Koran in condemning factionalism, he shows awareness of the problem. There is no way to view his Al Qaeda as anything but a forbidden faction or sect:

*Do not split up the religion by breaking into sects (6.159).*

**Verse of the Sword:** Bin-Laden cites the rough and tough, graphic "verse of the sword" (9.5) so as to justify the killing his Al Qaeda is engaged in. However, he fails to mention that the verse is followed by another (9.13) that shows that the Muslims were attacked first. Both bin-Laden and those who bash Islam effectively legitimize each other by citing the "verse of the sword," one to claim a license to kill and the other to criticize Islam for allowing it. Both are wrong, as Islam does stand for peace and fighting is allowed only after being attacked first:

*Fight and kill pagans wheresoever you find them, seize them as captives, beleaguer them, and lie in wait to ambush them (9.5). Fight those pagans who... attacked you first (9.13).*

*Fight in the way of Allah against those who fight against you, but do not begin the hostilities (2.190).*

**Being attacked first:** Knowing that Muslims must be attacked first but not wanting to directly state it, bin-Laden goes on to expresses his grievances against Jews and Christians in such a way as to make it seem that Islam was attacked. Building an American airbase at the request of the local government is deemed to be an attack, even though the local government does not consider it such.

America is said to be plundering the riches of Islam as it gives billions of dollars in aid to Egypt. America helps the Afghans, the Kuwaitis, and the Muslims in Kosovo and

Bosnia, and yet it is plundering and attacking. There is no logic, no reasoning, but just bin-Laden deeming things to be attacks. The statements are statements of conclusions, not of reasons. Bin Laden needs to do this for he must show Islam was attacked first, and this is all he can come up with.

**Jews and Christians:**  Bin-Laden also ignores the import of the verse of the sword (9.5) he cites. The verse applies only to pagans and thus automatically excludes Jews and Christians who are treated as believers in the Koran.  Bin Laden would never recognize the favorable treatment of Jew and Christians in the Koran.  He needs them as enemies and pagans so as to justify what he does, but the Koran treats them as believers, not as pagans:

*Whoever believes in God and the Last Day and does good, whether he be Muslim, Jew, Christian or Sabian, shall have their reward and should have no fear nor grieve on judgment day (2.62).*

**Individual duty:**  There is no individual duty to take up arms and kill as bin-Laden would have it.  Bin-Laden claims that throughout Islamic history the *ulama* unanimously agreed that jihad is an individual duty. Aside from it being inconceivable that the *ulama* ever unanimously agreed on anything, bin-Laden's having to refer to *ulama* "authority" shows that there is no support for it in the Koran.  The Koran wants consensus.  Where Muslims disagree or quarrel, the Koran creates a duty to make peace between them  --  so that they would be all together. The Koran strives for unity and consensus amongst Muslims, particularly when it comes to fighting:

*If parties of believers quarrel, make peace between them with fairness and justice. If one party does wrong to the other, fight the one who does wrong until they obey Allah (49.9).*

*All believers are brethren and you have a duty to make peace between your contending brethren (49.10).*

*Fight all together as they fight you all together; but know that Allah is with those who restrain themselves (9.36).*

*Keep your bond to Allah and be all together, not disunited (3.103).*

The consensus belongs to the community of Muslims or their legitimate government. Whether the legitimate government is religious or secular, those who do not obey would be in rebellion:

*Obey Allah and those in authority among you (4.59)*

The first caliph referred important matters, like a fighting jihad would be, to the Muslim community to decide. The Shiite recognize a delegation of authority to the Imam to declare a jihad. A fighting jihad was never an individual decision nor an effort to be pursued without the community being behind it. Allah protects sacred lives and places limitations on when Muslims could fight including the requirement of community consensus. It would be very inconsistent to allow a Muslim to individually declare his own fighting jihad and go out to kill people. There is no such individual duty as bin-Laden would like it to be.

If the community of Muslims did not decide fight, there would be a division or quarrel within the community if some Muslims continued to insist on fighting as their individual duty. Rather, each Muslim would have a duty to reconcile the differences. Stated another way, the individual Muslim has the duty to seek consensus, and not to decide on a jihad himself nor join a dissident group fighting a jihad without community consensus. The individual cannot force the community to fight, and he cannot decide to fight by himself without the community.

Bin Laden pays lip service to the Koran citing verse 9.36 about fighting all together, masterly weaving it into a deemed attack, while just having inconsistently said that Muslims have an individual duty to fight. Whether it is the erroneous individual duty to fight or correct fighting all together (with consensus) bin-Laden seems to stick on the side of fighting. Of course, bin-Laden omits the part of verse 9.36 where Allah calls for restraint:

*Fight all together as they fight you all together; but know that Allah is with those who restrain themselves (9.36).*

*Do not alter the words from their context nor neglect a portion of what the Koran says (5.13).*

Bin-Laden goes on, but it is time to go on to Hizbullah.

# Hizbullah's "Religious" War

Hizbullah is a terrorist organization engaged in a war against the State of Israel. It is also engaged in a struggle against other Muslims, as it was the one group that dissented in a Palestinian "cease-fire" conference held in Cairo in 2003. Hizbullah also stood up against a conference of Muslim nations that outlined a plan for peace in the Middle East in 2002. Surprisingly, Hizbullah was successful in torpedoing the Saudi Arabian lead effort, and the Saudi's desisted.

An explanatory book[11] delineates Hizbullah's positions and its anti-Judaic rationale based on the Koran. The book, most probably carefully vetted by Hizbullah, allowed me to check out the Koranic support Hizbullah claims it has.

All Jews are tainted according to Hizbullah even though the Koranic verses it cites contain language shows that there are good and bad amongst them. Most of the Koranic criticism of Jews comes from the exploration of the Torah, which Allah effective incorporates into Islam where the Koran does not override. The ancient Israelites were known to all to have disobeyed God, and they were

---

[11]   Amal Saad-Ghorayeb, *Hizbu'llah, Politics and Religion*, Pluto Press, London, 2002.

adequately punished for it as delineated in the Torah, with the Golden Calf being but one such incident. But that is not over and done with according to Hizbullah.

What could escape notice is that Hizbullah seizes upon the Koran's mentioning of the old criticisms, saying nothing new or telling. But, the Koran has a sort of balance to its criticisms, while Hizbullah concludes that God has demonized all Jews for all times. That clearly is not the case for in the end the Koran declares that Allah considers Jews to be believers and Allah will admit them to Paradise on the same basis as He admits Muslims. After all of Allah's criticism of the ancient Israelis as cited by Hizbullah, Allah still acknowledges He could reward Jews with Paradise when He sits in judgment:

*Whoever believes in God and the Last Day and does good, whether he be Muslim, Jew, Christian or Sabian, shall have their reward and should have no fear nor grieve on judgment day (2.62).*

Rather than demonization as Hizbullah would have it, the Koran spanks the Jews for the ancient disobedience as a kindly parent would punish his children and goes on from there to treat the children kindly and demand that others do so also.

In a number of verses not cited by Hizbullah, Allah clearly shows that individual determinations of guilt or evil must be made, and group condemnations are not condoned:

*There are good people amongst the Jews who speak the*

*truth and do justice with it (7.159).*
*People of a group are not all alike. There are those amongst the People of Book who are upright, believe in God and the Last Day and recite His messages throughout the night; they are righteous and their good deeds will not be denied them (3.113-5).*

This is devastating to Hizbullah position as their suicide attacks do not distinguish between individuals; they know that their attacks kill indiscriminately and sometimes also kill Muslims. Killing Muslims cannot be said to be accidental when Muslims should be known to be present in the vicinity where the bombs go off. Callous unconcern as to the presence of Muslims who are killed has to be the equivalent of intentional killing. That gets the severest condemnation from Allah, even His curse:

*Allah curses, and punishes with hell, whoever intentionally kills a believer (4.93).*

Muhammad's political battles with the three rebelling Jewish tribes of Medina are taken out of place and context and emphasized by Hizbullah as grounds for criticizing present day Jews. Hizbullah states that its conflict with Israel is a continuation of Muhammad's conflicts with the Jews of his day, and that Allah's damning of the Jews will last to the end of time (and thus include all future generations). But Allah did not damn the Jews and the Koran clearly holds a person responsible for only his or her own sins:

*Whoever helps a good cause will have its reward and*

*whoever helps an evil cause will bear the burdens of it (4.85).*
*Everyone will bear their own evil burdens in full on the day of judgment, and also the evil burdens of any unknowledgeable people they misled (16.25).*

The Torah, confirmed by Allah as being revealed by Him (3.3), states that the sins of the father will not be cast on the sons in all future generations. Muhammad having taken a Jewish wife (Safiyya) also contradicts Hizbullah claim that all Jews were forever damned. Thus, both the Koran and the Torah limit the carryover of sins, as did the act of Muhammad in taking a Jewish wife who had to be without sin, all in direct opposition to Hizbullah's position. The Koran is as clear as can be that the sins of the ancient Jews and Christians do not carry over to their children:

*The ancient Jews and Christians have passed away and theirs is what they had earned, while their progeny earn what is theirs and are not to be asked what their ancestors did (2.141).*

This is the most telling argument against Hizbullah's position. Hizbullah constantly seems to harp on what the Jews did in the ancient past (for which they were already punished by God) and attribute it all the way down to the present era so as to saddle present day Jews with it. But the Koran says they should not do that. There is no inherited sin in Islam according to the Koran, and Hizbullah contradicts the Koran.

Not only is one of Islam's basic themes (each person is responsible only for his her own actions) being violated, but a distinct verse of the Koran (2.141) specifically negates any current day responsibility for the actions of the ancient Jews and Christians. The entire structure of what Hizbullah says falls, and it is left only with way-out made-up positions.

The other way-out positions made-up by Hizbullah are clearly contradicted by history. For instance, Hizbullah claims that the Jews were not the original people of the Book (which is contradicted many times by the Koran), and that the Holocaust was a Jewish conspiracy and the gas chambers never existed (it being said to be a made-up ploy to elicit world sympathy, which is contradicted in history books around the world). Hizbullah also claims that Israeli parents have caused the death of their children by having moved to Palestine or by living there. It is not that Hizbullah killed those children. With this kind of logic, it is difficult to take anything Hizbullah says seriously.

Hizbullah also ignores the fact that the Arab Muslims are Semites and are thus joined with the Jews who are also Semites. Hizbullah could not let Nazi type anti-Semitism stand, lest they too fall into the net, so Hizbullah attempts to create a distinction between the Jewish race and the Jewish religion, as between them and Arabs and Islam. Hizbullah forgets that Ishmael and Isaac were brothers and have the same God:

*Muslims believe in Allah and the revelations in the Koran and in the revelations to Abraham, Ishmael, Isaac, Jacob and the tribes of Israel, Moses, Jesus, and all the other prophets, and do not distinguish between any of them (2.136).*

*Muslims should not argue with people of the Book in other than helpful ways, except for those of them who do wrong, and tell them that we Muslims believe in the revelations to us and in the revelations to you, and that our God and your God is the same one God (29.46).*

This also flies into the face of Hizbullah maintaining that it is the Jewish religion which is bad, and not the Semitic race. How can the Jewish religion be bad with the Koran treating Jews as believers? It seems particularly out of line to call the Jewish religion bad with Allah have revealed it:

*Allah has revealed the Koran to you, and verifies that He also revealed the Torah and Gospel* (3.3).

Hizbullah goes on to criticize "innate Jewishness," whatever that means. Hizbullah taints Jews with illusory racial superiority as claiming to be chosen by God and pyramids that in causing the Jews to kill gentiles and slay Prophets. That, they say, proves that a people with such aggression, depravity and shedding of blood cannot now be trusted to now make peace with Arabs. Hizbullah ignores that the Koran similarly called Muslims an exalted nation and that is was Allah who revealed the Jews were chosen, chosen by Allah just like He was later to choose Muslims:

*This day Allah perfected your religion for you and completed His favor to you by choosing Islam as your religion (5.3).*
*Allah has chosen you for His religion and has named you Muslims (22.78).*
*Allah has made Muslims an exalted nation in the middle of the world and a teacher of nations (2.143).*

Difficult and obtuse theological positions arise from Hizbullah's circular reasoning. Acknowledging that no one and no group is born evil, it nevertheless insists that all future generations of Jews will carry the blame of the ancient Jews. With neither the Koran (2.141) nor the Torah[12] forever saddling sins on those who did not commit them, Hizbullah's is simply making up its own theology.

This goes on and one. Hizbullah notices the Koranic criticism of rabbis not reigning in the Jews (5.63). By failing to prevent evil-speaking, Hizbullah concludes that the rabbis are themselves essentially evil. Here Hizbullah doesn't pick on Christians, nor for that matter pick on the

---

[12]   The Book of Exodus 20.5 saddles iniquities of fathers upon their children until the "third and fourth" generation of them. "Third and fourth" is curious language for either would be very limited, suggesting it refers to the number of generations possibly alive at the same time, normally three but occasionally four. Thus, sin could only taint living generations in Judaism. That would apply in Islam as it was a revelation of Allah, but it was abrogated by Allah in 2.141 so that there is no carryover of sin at all in Islam.

Muslim *ulama* for not reigning in the Kharijite murder of Ali (Muhammad's son-in-law), the Umayyad massacre of Hussein (Muhammad's grandson), or the Wahhabi destruction of Hussein's shrine or the innumerable times the moderate *ulama* failed to reign in Islamic extremists.

In criticizing the three Jewish tribes Muhammad had trouble with, and trying to show Muhammad hated Jews, Hizbullah has to confront Muhammad having married a Jewess. Hizbullah has to acknowledge that marrying Jews is sanctioned by the Koran, but here it inserts its own theology forbidding marriage to Jews. Apparently, the Koran can be varied by Hizbullah whenever it wants to do so. And yet Hizbullah claims that the Koran is its constitution, which doesn't square with the apparent ease in which it disregards what the Koran says.

In the end, it appears that Hizbullah dredges up whatever it can find to criticize Jews and Judaism so as to avoid acknowledging that its antagonism is really based ib political opposition to the State of Israel. Hizbullah cannot concede that its struggle against Israel is politically based and had no religious underpinnings in Islam.

Thus, it is crucial for Hizbullah to present the current conflict against the Jews as a continuation of the old Islamic intolerance of Jews, which intolerance never existed. Without support, that position is maintained, and there is no explanation how the old transgressions are transferred down to today, other than by pure slander. And that also slanders Islam which has been the most tolerant of religions, even of Jews, especially of Jews and Christians.

As a strictly political matter, one could understand the Hizbullah struggle against Israel. There have always been political differences between nations and they will exist to the end of time unless man evolves mechanisms to substitute dialogue, compromise and agreement for war. That mechanism was supposed to be the United Nations, but it itself became another political battleground.

States have always fought wars for political purposes, but it is unusual for a political group like Hizbullah to declare war on a state, so they attempt to recast themselves and the war into a religious mold. Not all terrorist groups do this, as some acknowledge that what they do is political, but, apparently, religion attracts more recruits in Islam and makes it easier to find suicide bombers.

One is surprised to see how little support Hizbullah actually has in the Koran for its religious vendetta. As a result, the wonder becomes whether Hizbullah really believes what it says and is deceiving itself, or whether it does not believe its rhetoric and is deliberately deceiving others. Either way, the Koran is being disobeyed:

*Be steadfast in fair dealing, and do not let hatred of a people induce you into doing wrong and depart from justice (5.8).*

# A Brief History of Early Islam

The early, formative years of Islam have been depicted in different ways. Devout Muslims, who heard and passed-on the oral transmissions of the day, have their own versions. These versions likely include both accurate historical portrayals and also fancied portrayals tailored to what the transmitters perceived through their own glasses.

Modern scientists (historians, archeologists, linguists and others) who sifted through the evidence of centuries also have a variety of views. They include some surprising ones like it was all made-up with the Prophet Muhammad never existing, or that the religion was created after the conquest of the Arabian Peninsula so as to provide some glue to hold the conquest together. Most of the modern versions were by Western scientists. It has been suggested that Muslim scientists refuse to explore the area, being content to leave religious beliefs as they are. So am I.

What follows is how I piece together Islam's early

history. While I am fascinated by the scientific work, I feel that the history as accepted by the devout must form the core of this historical review as long as it is reasonable to do so. I pick and choose amongst the devout versions and cull them at will so as to present this very brief portrayal. Thus, what follows is simply how I see it.

## THE KABA, THE HOLIEST SHRINE OF ISLAM

I start my historical story with the Kaba (or Kabah), the ancient structure at the core of Islam. It is the shrine that should be visited in a pilgrimage (the *hajj)* by every Muslim at least once a lifetime, a Koranic requirement and one of the pillars of Islam. The Kaba is located in the Sacred Mosque in the city of Mecca in present day Saudi Arabia. All Muslims, wherever located on the globe must pray in its direction, having replaced the direction of Jerusalem that was initially used by Muslims:

*Wherever you are, turn your faces to the Sacred Mosque when you pray (2.144).*
*Muslims cannot follow the direction of prayer of the People of the Book (2.145).*
*Perform the pilgrimage to the Sacred Mosque in the service of Allah (2.196).*

The Kaba is the holiest shrine of Islam, a cubical building (under 50 x 50 feet) in a courtyard about ten times that in the central mosque in Mecca, the Sacred Mosque. The structure contains a sacred black corner stone, an unhewn stone from a mountain or, as some maintain, a meteorite. Somewhere in the very distant past, somebody or some cult must have built an architecturally simple building around the unusual stone and made it a shrine where the stone was worshipped, and where idols of one sort or another were placed.

The structure predated the time of Abraham and, being on the trade routes, was initially used for pagan idol worship. Tradition has it that Abraham and Ishmael rebuilt it. The Koran associates Abraham and Ishmael with the Kaba:

*Allah has made the Kaba, the Sacred House, a secure asylum for the people (5.97).*

*Allah made His House a safe place for men to meet and pray in the place Abraham prayed after he and Ishmael cleared all the idols (2.125).*

The Kaba might have been amongst the first structures for worship in the world, or at least the oldest surviving after reconstructions. The time of Abraham is, say, about 2000 BCE. Distinct religious belief systems may have been rare in the very early days, but it is clear that people did make and use idols, indicating that religions existed. The Kaba became a place where those idols could be put.

Later the Kaba was said to have become a shrine used by Christians working the trade routes and, still later, the Arab Quraysh tribe of Mecca became its owner and protector. Fees were collected from visitors to the Kaba, and the Quraysh became wealthy and one of the dominant tribes of Mecca. That was the tribe of Muhammad.

But the Kaba was not to become the holiest shrine of Islam until many years later when the religion had a fairly sizeable community of believers and had fought a major battle. That was years after the *hijra* in 622, the date of Muhammad's pilgrimage from Mecca to Medina some two hundred miles to the north. When he went to Medina, Muhammad's followers numbered less than a hundred.

Up to that time, Muhammad and his followers prayed in the direction of Jerusalem, which was to the northwest. Muhammad then received Allah's revelation and recited to the congregation. Allah had changed the direction of prayer and wanted them to pray in the direction of Mecca and the Kaba, which was south of Medina.

The history of the Kaba says much about how intertwined Islam was with the prior monotheistic religions, and in particular in its relationship with Judaism. Much scientific scholarly research supports this, and it quite apparent from reading the Koran itself.

The Jewish relationship seems to have ebbed and flowed, as in changing the direction of prayer from Jerusalem to Mecca, but it was always there and always strong. Jerusalem had been the original Muslim direction of worship and it was switched to the Kaba which also had a Jewish relationship in that Abraham was first mentioned in the Jewish Torah. The Patriarch Abraham visited the Kaba with his son Ishmael. The Koran says they raised the foundation, although it could have been part of rebuilding the Kaba. Some would say that all the references in the Koran to Judaism demonstrate that Islam is partly rooted there.

The Muslim view is that Islam had its own separate track, starting with Abraham. Abraham became the first Muslim, was closely connected with Islam's most sacred shine, and founded the most sacred Islamic city, Mecca. Thus, both Islam and Judaism claim the Patriarch Abraham as being their own. Islam's claim was there from the very beginning, not rooted in anything else:

*Abraham asked Allah to make the region of Mecca a secure city of peace and feed its people (2.126).*

*Abraham and Ishmael raised the foundations of the Kaba, the House of God, and asked Allah to accept it from them (2.127).*

*Abraham and Ishmael asked Allah to make them Muslims and make from their offspring a nation submissive to Allah (2.128).*

Muhammad was born in Mecca, and had very close ties to the Kaba. His grandfather was said to be the owner and guardian of the Kaba, or the caretaker of it. Muhammad was said to have rebuilt the Kaba just after the time a snake was said to have take possession of the walls of the Kaba. There is no scientific evidence as to these speculations or stories, nor does any of it appear in the Koran.

It should also be noted that there was no Mosque as such in Mecca at the time of Muhammad. A Mosque need not be a very formal building; it can be only a courtyard used for prayer, and the area around the Kaba would qualify. But the Muslims were few and after the *hijra* were all in Medina. At that time, the Kaba probably reverted to being used as a place of worship by idolaters and was full of idols.

One of the reasons given for Muhammad having been driven out of Mecca by his own tribe, the Quraysh, was the significant loss of income from the cessation of visits by idolaters to the Kaba that would result if Islam were to replace idolatry. The possibility that the Kaba would become a place for Islamic pilgrimages, and replace or increase their income, did nothing for the Quraysh as they continued to send troops to fight Muhammad.

There is much speculation as to why a place of pre-Islamic Arab paganism was so honored in Islam. But the Kaba was honored, however not to the level of considering it to have divine attributes. Muslims honor the Kaba as the spiritual center of Islam and do not worship it; the black stone is not an idol and kissing it is not a remnant of idolatry.

# HOW DO THREE RELIGIONS HAVE THE SAME ABRAHAM AS THEIR FOUNDER?

I was initially confused as to how three religions, Judaism, Christianity and Islam, could have the same founding Patriarch, Abraham. I would like to share how I reconciled things to my personal satisfaction in case you are wondering about the same thing.

After Abraham left Ishmael in Mecca, he returned north to Canaan/Palestine and his other son Isaac and resumed life in the North. Ishmael remained in Mecca, which was south of Canaan/Palestine. The brothers, Ishmael and Isaac led their separate lives in the North and the South and their seed grew into nations. Isaac's progeny in the North, took over the Promised Land, and were called the Israelites or Jews. Ishmael's progeny in the South remained in Arabia and were called Arabs or Muslims.

The time of Abraham was about 2000 BCE, give or take a few centuries because there no archeological evidence to be found. The Jews wrote their story about Abraham, starting about 1000 BCE, from the ancient oral transmissions and that became the Torah and later the Hebrew Bible. The Hebrew Bible was adopted by the Christians when they came on the scene, making it part of their Scripture and calling it the Old Testament. Abraham is the Patriarch of the Jews in the Torah and since Christianity includes that heritage in its Old Testament, Abraham is also the Patriarch of Christianity.

The Koran comes on the scene much later and tells the story of Abraham and Ishmael back when they were in Arabia in about the same 2000 BCE time frame, at which time Abraham and Ishmael became the first Muslims. But the Koran wasn't written as the Torah had been written, carrying the genealogy of the people forward from the time of Abraham.

The Koran does not record the ancient oral transmissions starting from the time of Abraham and Ishmael, nor does it bring the genealogy of the Arabs/Muslims forward from that time. The Koran basically speaks from the time Muhammad and the revelations to him, which included the revelations as to Abraham and Ishmael.

The oral transmissions of the people in the South as to their history were either lost or replaced when the oral tradition began to focus on the recitals of Muhammad beginning in 610 CE. The Koran goes all the way back to the Creation by referring to the Torah, but the Koran itself picks up with Abraham and Ishmael. Abraham is the Patriarch of Islam because he was the first Muslim, not because of any reference to the Jewish tradition.

And thus you have Abraham as the founding father of all three religions, Judaism, Christianity and Islam, which take his name as the Abrahamic religions.

## THE REVELATION AND WRITING OF THE KORAN

Islam it is the only religion said to have developed in the full light of history, using the *hijra* in 622 CE as the starting point. That is year 1 of the Islamic calendar, year 622 of the Christian calendar, and year 4383 of the Jewish calendar.[13] The older religions were recorded in writing well after the events. The Koran was written and collated almost contemporaneously with Allah's revelations to Muhammad.

The Koran did not come from Muhammad as a finished product. In the year 610, when Muhammad was age 40, Muhammad began hearing the revelations of Allah through the voice of the angel Gabriel. This continued for more than two decades until Muhammad's death in 632. How the revelations were handled by Muhammad is not clear.

Some say that Muhammad was unschooled but nevertheless recorded the revelations in writing, making the endeavor all the more wondrous for the devout. It is unlikely that he was unschooled, being from one of the richest families in Mecca, even then a leading city. It is

---

[13]  The Islamic calendar dates from when Muhammad fled Mecca and went to Medina. The Jewish calendar is reckoned from the traditional date of the Creation. The Christian or Gregorian calendar dates from about the birth of Jesus.

also unlikely that he wrote the revelations as it seems that Muhammad recited the revelations aloud and there were people at his feet when he did so.

The people at his feet could have included scribes, rare in those days for not many could read and write. Writing materials were scarce and expensive. But there were some writings on parchment, leather, bones of animals, and parts of trees, the usual writing materials of that age. Paper wasn't yet available in Arabia. It was likely that many more people, who could not read and write, heard the recitals and committed them to memory. The oral tradition was very strong in those days.

It took another two decades after the death of Muhammad to assemble the writings that could be found, listen to the oral testimony of those who survived the wars, and compile what is now the Koran. The writings, mostly scraps and pieces, were said to have been destroyed after the compilers were finished with the Koran. The early private versions containing variations from the official Koran were burned. With the propensity of believers to collect relics being likely even back then, and with nothing ever being found, it does seem that the written source materials were so destroyed, and thus the absence of any "hard" evidence.

Some 42 years passed from the first revelation in 610 to the final compilation of the Koran, a record for Scripture.

The New Testament took some 300 years and the Hebrew Bible/Old Testament over 600 years from the time the oral transmissions were first reduced to writing.


## A BIRD'S EYE VIEW OF THE EARLY HISTORY

Islam was born in the 7<sup>th</sup> century, dated to the year-622 when the Prophet Muhammad (who born in 570) departed Mecca for Medina to practice the new faith in a more hospitable area and become the secular head of the conflicted community in Medina.

During the 10 year period from fleeing to Medina to his death in 632, Muhammad and his generals were phenomenally successful in conquering the Arabian Peninsula.  Still without the Koran, which was finally compiled in about 652, Muhammad's successors continued the astonishing successes in moving beyond Arabia.

Islam moved north to conquer Palestine and Syria, west to conquer Egypt, and north/east to conquer Iraq and Persia (Iran), as they are known today.  By the end of the 8<sup>th</sup> century, Islam had also conquered the lands bordering on Mediterranean Europe, North Africa and the Levant, extending its reach almost to China, the Upper Nile, Spain and further.

The Dome of the Rock was built about 692, a year

after Jerusalem was captured. It was deliberately placed on the very location most important to Jews and the spot Muslims had previously faced in prayer. It was the location of the Jewish Temple destroyed by the Romans and the place where Abraham was said to have offered to sacrifice Isaac, Ishmael's younger brother.

The significance of this could not have been greater for the ultimate triumph of Islam over both Judaism and Christianity. The Dome of the Rock sat over the Church of the Holy Sepulcher, the location where Christ had been buried. That was the high point of Muslim unity. There was only one community of Muslins and not much of an *ulama*, the learned ones who later broke into sects and so changed Islam through internal strife.

For a couple of centuries, Islam was the "light of the world," the unquestioned leader in science, literature, art including architecture, and philosophy, while the Christian dominated Europe was in the dark ages. The growing *ulama* began to oppress Islamic society, gradually extinguishing the "light of the world."

The three Abrahamic religions (Judaism, Christianity and Islam) lived in harmony in a tolerant Islam until the European Christians mounted the Crusades, killing thousands and thousands of Muslims and Jews in and about Jerusalem.

By the end of the 12<sup>th</sup> century, Jerusalem was recaptured from the Christians but, by then, the Christian West was starting to come out of the dark ages. In the next three centuries, with acceleration at the time of the renaissance, the West drove ahead on all scientific and intellectual fronts and also originated an age of intolerance against both Jews and Muslims.

But yet, during this time, Islam was adopted far and wide outside Arabia, to the point that Arabia and Arabs represents only an minor portion of Islam. The majority of Muslims now reside in Asia in countries where they dominate, like Indonesia, Pakistan and Bangladesh, and in countries where they are significant minorities like India (over 100 million Muslims) and the Philippines. In addition, there are the non-Arab Muslim countries of Turkey and Iran, and many countries in Africa. Perhaps one of six people in the world is Muslim, a tremendous success for the religion if not for the first Muslim countries themselves that had fallen further behind the West.

The very early wars of Islam were wars of expansion, essentially wars for spoils and booty with religious conversions playing little or no part in it. In the later years, when the extremist *ulama* came into their own, a religious purpose in some conquests started to appear. Religious internal or civil wars became commonplace. Few of these wars find support in the Koran as just wars. Islam was violent, but the Koran does stand for peace;    thus a disconnect becomes apparent, courtesy of the extremist *ulama*.

The pre-Islamic tribal history of Arabia highlighted the prevalence of fighting during those ancient days, not much different than in tribal lands anywhere. The tribes were essentially communities where people lived in peace and presented a unified face to the outer world. Larger or fiercer tribes conquered the weaker ones and had the incentive to preserve the lives of the conquered, as allies or slaves, so that they would help protect against still larger tribes. Even without conquests, there were alliances where tribes agreed not to attack each other or not attack the other's trade routes, and agreed to mutual defense.

Such was the situation when the tribes of Medina asked Muhammad to come and make peace amongst them, and then lead them, with all the tribes agreeing to fight together if Medina was attacked. It was that agreement that gave Muhammad the force he used to fight the Meccans who attacked him in Medina.

The "protector" system was in full bloom -- the stronger protected the weaker in exchange for aid and assistance when needed. Individuals also had "protectors" within the same tribe even though tribal members were not supposed to fight one another. Apparently there were no religious or ethical compulsions against killing in those days, or, if they existed, they weren't very deep.

It was a matter of strength or protection, with the "protector" deterring killing because of the implicit threat of revenge, and actually following through on it.  In a sense, Muhammad was protected within his clan.  He was an outcast because of his beliefs, but he couldn't be touched because he had one or more powerful protectors within the clan.  When the protection was withdrawn, he apparently had no option but flee.

Many groups or tribes could live together in peace in a city, frequently behind walls that made it a fortress against attack from others.  The city was a community, but the tribe was the unit that had the basic allegiance of its members.

Scientific/historical evidence is basically lacking as to that age in Arabia.  There weren't many people who knew how to write.  The oral tradition was as reliable as oral transmissions from generation to generation could be.  They were probably made more dubious as the storytellers on the street corners, the entertainment source of that age, competed for customers by embellishing stories.

The periods to be covered in more detail include:

| | |
|---|---|
| 622-632 | Muhammad, the political ruler. |
| 632-660 | Four righteous caliphs. |
| 660-750 | Umayyad dynasty of oppression. |
| 750-1055 | Abbasid dynasty of more oppression. |
| 1055-1258 | Turks, Ayyubid dynasty & Crusades. |
| 1258 on | Mongols, Ottoman & the West. |

## MUHAMMAD, THE POLITIAL RULER (622-632)

As I piece it together, it would appear that Muhammad's proselytizing in Mecca upset the community of idol worshippers who used and financially benefited from the Kaba. Muhammad's preaching opposed idol worshipping. When his personal "protection" was withdrawn by his own Quraysh tribe, Muhammad fled Mecca so as to avoid attack by the bigger and wealthier Umayyad tribe and also by members of his own tribe who owned the Kaba. He went to Medina, a backward area that was in array, and was welcomed as a force who could forge peace amongst the warring factions.

He did this, forming a community amongst the disparate groups; a political community and not a religious one since the great majority of Medina residents did not then accept Islam. Not having any means of support, Muhammad and his followers began raiding Meccan caravans. This might be viewed from Muhammad's perspective as just retaliation for being driven from his home in Mecca, and from the Meccan perspective as an offense against his own tribe and Mecca in general.

Mecca retaliated by sending its army against Muhammad, and Muhammad defended by calling on his contractual allies for help in repulsing the attackers. His allies, including three Jewish tribes, contributed hundreds of troops to fight alongside the less than 100 Muslims. In

624, Mohammad's army brilliantly defeated the larger attacking force from Mecca at a place called Badr. It was a place and event to be remembered because it was the single most important battle fought by Islam -- the continued existence of the religion depended on it. It was a terrible battle, with fathers on both sides fighting their own sons on the other side.

Power begets opposition and some of Muhammad's own allies, including three Jewish tribes that had supported Mohammad, later had to be subdued. The opponents feared that Mohammad was getting too strong politically; it had nothing to do with religion. The expulsion of two Jewish tribes in 625 was peaceable, but the third was destroyed in a deadly war in 627. This too appeared to be a political act, without religious motivation.

The tribes of Mecca continued to attack Muhammad. Muhammad was defeated at Uhud in 625 and was successful in the trench war of 627. It was called the battle of the trench because Muhammad's men dug a trench that made the enemy's cavalry ineffective. It is to be noted that by the year 627, Muhammad was strong enough to come back from the Uhud defeat in 625. Had the battle of Badr a year early in 624 been lost, it is not at all clear Muhammad would have been able to recoup. After the 627 battle, Muhammad with his new sizeable cavalry became very strong, powerful enough for his armies to eventually subdue the rest of Arabia.

In response to an attack by the Mecca tribes on a tribe allied with Muhammad, in the year 630 Muhammad sent a strong force against Mecca. Mecca surrendered peacefully. It did not then adopt Islam, nor was it forced to do so, but it eventually came around. So too it was in the rest of Arabia with the wars being fought in the old tribal traditions of conquest and booty until Arabia was pacified. The wars were not religiously driven wars. Muhammad died in 632.

As pieced together, this history shows that Muhammad believed in the Koranic declaration that force should not be used to expand the religion. Muhammad never imposed Islam on his captives. The wars were essentially politically and economically (booty) based.

The so-called "religious wars" of Muhammad didn't exist. Contrary to popular opinion in the West, it was never the sword in one hand and the Koran in the other, at least not initially under Muhammad. Nor could these wars have been religious wars as the religion was not firmly implanted, as shown by the danger that the Arabian tribes fighting for booty would disband after the death of Muhammad.

The succession to Muhammad became a bone of contention. Some Muslims favored succession through Muhammad's family and some through Muhammad's tribe. Some Muslims favored those who first adopted Islam and their heirs, while some favored those who welcomed and housed the Prophet in Medina and their heirs.  Some merely favored the most pious Muslim, and some had split views.  Each had supporting rationales and Islam was on its way to factionalization, although consensus was obtained for the first and second caliphs.


## THE FOUR CALIPHS (632-660)

The first caliph was Abu Bakr, who at that time had complete secular authority and shared religious authority. Muhammad had complete secular and religious authority, but he was the Prophet and the last of the prophets.

Abu Bakr was the first of four caliphs who were companions of Muhammad, all but one being of Muhammad's Quraysh tribe.  Abu Bakr had been perhaps the oldest and closest companion of Muhammad, and may have been the unanimous choice as Muhammad gave no succession indication and had no surviving sons.

Abu Bakr ruled from 632 to 634, dying of natural causes, and did little more than keep together the community forged by Muhammad.  After Muhammad's death, some tribes revolted for political and economic reasons because their ties were primarily with Muhammad as a military leader able to deliver spoils and booty.  Many if not most of the tribes never accepted Islam as a religion. To keep the renegades in the community, Abu Bakr let the war games continue by allowing raids into non-Arabian lands. While reputed to be of limited talent, Abu Bakr appears to have done a good job of holding Islam together.

The second caliph, Umar ibn al-Khattab (ruled 634 to 644), was very different than his predecessor. Umar was said to be the strong, talented and aggressive force behind the conservative Muhammad and the Muslim community recognized that. He may well have been the unsung hero of Islam, dwarfed by the overriding stature of Muhammad.

Umar continued the sport of fighting for booty since it was the only available means of supplementing meager Arab incomes. As Muslims, Arabs could no long attack members of their own community and the largely barren Arabian lands didn't produce much. The lands of Palestine, Syria, Egypt, Iraq and parts of Persia and North Africa happened to then be ready for conquest for a number of reasons, and found themselves under Muslim control by the time Umar was assassinated in 644.

It was during Umar's 10-year reign that the compilation of the Koran was undertaken, and the religion finally took form. Umar needed the unity of religion to keep his community, and his armies, together. They were forming an Islamic community of Arabs of the entire Arabian Peninsula, and perfecting their own religion for themselves.

The newly conquered, non-Arabian lands were held somewhat apart. They had more Jews and Christians, people of the Book having similar beliefs, but Islam was being viewed as a religion for Arabs. Arabs were the descendents of Ishmael, while Judaism and Christianity belonged to the descendants of Isaac. Attempts to convert the conquered people were not made for another 100 years or so. The newly conquered lands became under the rule and "protection" of the Muslims.

A form of the old "protector" system was used as a system of protecting and controlling the conquered people. A poll a tax was to be paid as a form of spoils, paid for protection against others, and paid so as to acknowledge subservience to the Muslims. The protected people (called *dhimmi*) were protected against raids and avenged if harmed. It was an outstanding example of Islam's religious tolerance at that time, underscored by enlightened political and economic rationale.

Thus, the newly conquered nations were handled in a farsighted and unique way; towns were neither destroyed nor deliberately wrecked. The old residents were left where they were, and were free to practice their faiths and govern themselves as long as they paid the poll tax. The tax created a long-term income stream at the cost of losing the captured peoples as additions to the Muslim war machine. That wasn't considered much of a loss. The Muslim armies were phenomenally successful without the *dhimmi*, and they weren't wanted or needed. It was far better to get a steam of income.

There was no effort to convert the conquered people as they were not the descendants of Ishmael; that is, they were not Arabs. In the conquered lands, the conquering Muslims kept apart, building what might be called garrison towns for themselves where Islam was practiced. For example, the city of Basra in Iraq and Qum in Iran were originally Muslim garrison towns.

The third caliph, who took over in 644 upon Umar's assassination, was Uthman ibn Affan, a son-in-law of Muhammad. Uthman captured more lands East and West, and largely continued the practice of not being too persistent in occupying the new lands and not being on a religious crusade. However, grumbling started within the Muslim ranks and this soon led to conflict and division in Islam.

The Muslim elite claimed to be angry about the lack of spoils, booty and land additions, and yet the situation had been largely the same under the popular Umar. The real anger was that Uthman was of the Umayyad[14] clan and not

---

[14] The Umayyad clan was actually part of the Quraysh tribe, as was Muhammad's clan. However, the two clans were in opposition to one another. Viewing the Umayyads as a tribe separate from the Muhammad's Quraysh tribe simplifies matters.

of Muhammad's Quraysh clan. Uthman appointed Umayyads to positions of responsibility, and in particular, he appointed an individual who Muhammad had viewed as his chief opponent in Mecca. Uthman was assassinated in 656 by a group of Muslim soldiers and they took it upon themselves to appoint the fourth caliph.

The fourth caliph was Ali bin Abi Talib (ruled 656 to 660), a closer son-in-law of Muhammad and he was of Muhammad's clan. Ali had married Fatima, Muhammad's favorite daughter. Ali was immediately caught up in crossfire.

The Umayyad's naturally felt that Ali should punish Uthman's murderers, Uthman having been a member of their clan. The other clans felt that Uthman was an unjust ruler and such punishment would be unwarranted. Ali retreated to a garrison town in Iraq, where he had much personal support, and made it his capital. That area later became the home of the Shiites.

Wars and intrigue followed, and Ali was murdered in 660 by an extremist *ulama* group, the Kharijite, who had their own religious views. This was not a "normal" political assassination. It had a religious base and religious motives. The extremist *ulama* had come into their own. Islam was off to some serious internal strife.

## UMAYYAD DYNASTY OF OPPRESSION (660-750)

By this time, the *ulama* were well established, and they split into groups. Some of the *ulama* might properly be blamed for supporting division in Islam (in violation of Koranic demands), and the rest of the *ulama* properly blamed for <u>not</u> forging unity (in accordance with Koranic demands).

The decline, whether it started with the Kharijite *ulama* or other *ulama* before then, could be attributed to the *ulama* splitting off into sects, each trying to impose their views on others as the Kharijite did in murdering Ali. How different Islam would look today had there been an effective peace and unity contingent amongst the *ulama*.

The murder of Ali in 660 ushered in a new era for Islam. The age of the caliphate was over and dynasties started to rule Islam. Internal strife grew, leading to a longing for the early 7th century Muslim ideals. The ideal was Muslim unity without internal division and strife according to the dictates of the Koran, not necessarily the ideal of an agrarian society. In a sense, the ideal was of a society before the *ulama* became powerful and without the strife created by the extremists amongst the *ulama*.

The age of the caliphates sowed many of the seeds of future civil conflict in Islam. Many Muslims had felt that Ali should have been the first caliph. Ali was the husband of Fatima, the Prophet's favored daughter.   With the Prophet having no living sons, Ali was considered the Prophet's closest male relative.  Ali's murder and the still later wars and murders of Ali's heirs created the schism in the Arab world between the Shiite, who are the followers of Ali, and the Sunni representing the rest of the Arabs.

Ali had relocated to Iraq and Iran and that area became the Shiite homeland.  The major Shiite shrines are in Iraq, in Najaf where Ali's shrine is located, and in Karbala, the locale of the Umayyad massacre of Hussein ibn Ali, Ali's son and Muhammad's grandson.  Those wounds never healed.  Had there been an effective *ulama* insisting on unity, those wounds would probably not have been allowed to happen in the first place or have been quickly healed. Had there been no *ulama* at all, there probably would have been no atrocities.

The caliphate also brought out the different views as to how Islam was to be governed.  Initially, the caliph was to be chosen by the ordinary Muslim community and that community was to be consulted on important religious matters.  At first the *ulama* substituted themselves for the larger community of Muslims for consensus and consultation, and later groups of *ulama* divided into forbidden sects and each began to impose their views on others as the Kharijite did in murdering Ali.  The pattern of disregarding or disobeying the Koran was thus established -- established by some of those in the *ulama*, the learned men, the scholars, the doctors of law and the other self-appointed and so-called religious leaders.

The Kharijite would be illustrative of scores of such sects plaguing Islam starting in those ancient days. The Kharijite assassinated Ali because they thought Uthman didn't deserve to be murdered and Ali had no right to compromise on punishing his murders. Later, a Kharijite leader took the position that Muslims who did not go out to fight with them in the rebellions they were conducting could be considered a non-Muslim and summarily killed.

This has become a familiar ploy used by today's extremist *ulama* and terrorists. Recognizing that they would be disregarding the Koran by killing fellow Muslims, they merely deem those Muslims that they would kill to be non-Muslims.

The Umayyad clan took over after Ali was murdered in 660, using force buttressed by their wealth, and established the first of the Arab dynasties. They moved the capital to Damascus -- for the first time clearly leaving the Arabian Peninsula and the world of Muhammad -- a humiliation to Arabia as if it were no longer worthy.

There is nothing specific on a dynasty in the Koran. However, a dynasty would seem to run afoul of equality concepts since the son of the ruler is deemed to more equal than anyone else and deserves to succeed the father. But this might well go too far because the Koran does recognize monarchies and this is what monarchies do.

The Umayyad caliphate went from father to son until 750, as contrasted to the first four caliphs where there was no father to son succession.  At first, the Umayyad caliphs followed the Muhammad model of austerity and a hands-on approach to ruling, but soon enough became remote absolute monarchs with splendorous wealth.

The wealth of Islam in that period would, in accordance with a "riches" theory, create leisure for a segment of the population;  giving them the time to explore and allowing the freedom of mind to do so.  This later led to Islam's spectacular rise in the arts and sciences.  At the same time, the increasing power of the *ulama* was leading to greater religious restrictiveness, which restrictiveness they started to impose on the secular society to the point of oppressiveness.  As it played out in the following centuries, the one led to Islam becoming the light of the world and the other led to the extinguishment of the light.

External expansion and conquests continued, but still Islam did not encourage conversions, being content to treat Islam as a religion for Arabs and satisfied with earning the *dhimmi* poll tax.  When Islam lost an important battle in Constantinople, that Eastern avenue of expansion into Europe was blocked.  Islam's Western expansion up through Africa and extended to Spain came to an end in a lost battle in 732. European expansion was at an end, but of little concern for the booty in that backward part of the world wasn't worth the candle, or so it was rationalized.

While religion didn't drive Islamic expansion, the spoils of war did and that was important as Islam had essentially little productive capacity. By about 720, conversions were encouraged so as to build the Muslim communities, but at the expense of losing the poll tax. The conquered people (*dhimmi*) had been treated well, had acclimated to Islam and liked the opportunity to avoid the poll tax with the result that they flocked to convert to Islam. As it turned out for the most part in the early years, the Koranic dictate that no force should be used in expanding the religion prevailed.

The diverse views of the *ulama* continued to make secular rule very difficult. The old succession battles still fomented trouble, as did allegations that the Umayyad rulers weren't pious enough, or that Muhammad had done this or that in similar circumstances. And the converts to Islam didn't quite find the equal treatment required by the Koran. Dissatisfaction increased, revolts and uprisings became more frequent and another clan saw the chance to gain control.

The Abbasids, essentially from the Shiite areas of Iraq and Iran, won a number of battles and became the victor in 750, being helped by their claims of being descendants of

Muhammad.   Again, it was the quest for political power under the guise of religion, but this time it was the political elite instead of the *ulama* using religion as a tool to gain power.


## ABBASID DYNASTY, MORE OPPRESSION (750-1055)

The Abbasids were murderous, killing the Umayyads and a fair number of Shiites as well so as to solidify their position.    All reference to the Muhammad model disappeared;   it was a new dynasty of absolute monarchs who insisted on prostrations and acted as gods or Allah's representative.  Internal strife grew and was subdued.  The splendor of the court grew exponentially as did the harems, notwithstanding the Koran limiting Muslims to no more than four wives.

The capital was moved to Baghdad.   After all opposition was brutally crushed, there was a period of peace and prosperity.  The Abbasid Caliph Harun al-Rashid (ruled from 786 to 809) actively fostered the arts and sciences and helped move Islam toward becoming the light of the world.   The new converts (former *dhimmi*) participated significantly by translating scientific and philosophical texts from their native languages and traveling to obtain new texts and language skills.

The *ulama* also continued to develop during the

Abbasid dynasty. More schools of religious thought, including some mysticism, appeared and further factionalized Muslim society into still more sects. The loosely knit *ulama* started to develop some structure as schools of jurisprudence appeared and the compilations of the hadiths neared completion, each school sponsoring their own compilation.

The hadiths were to become very important as being the key component of the new Islamic law (the Shariah), the other part being minor portions of the Koran which actually had little secular "law" in it. The hadiths essentially represented an extensive body of secular practices, containing rules on how just about everything was to be done, using Muhammad as the model although he had died some 200 years earlier.

The *ulama* were the interpreters of the Shariah and naturally became the jurists. There were many schools of jurisprudence, but most fell by the wayside as four schools became foremost. The ranks of the jurists greatly expanded the ranks of the old doctors of law, and they added to the other learned men and scholars who made up the *ulama*. All did their part to exercise power and control over the community of ordinary Muslims, who, according to the Koran, were to rule the secular through their governments and consensus amongst themselves.

The *ulama* became the administrators and judges for

250

the Abbasids. The Abbasids accepted the concept of the Shariah controlling everything, excepting only themselves. The Abbasids and the *ulama* worked together and supported each other; each to give the other legitimacy in the eyes of the public. This was to be the pattern of the future in tyrannical governments.

It turned out that the Shariah would do in the Abbasids. Adoption of the Shariah delivered secular law making and administration into the hands of the *ulama*. The *ulama* grabbed religious control. They swayed the masses to the point where nobody dared to disagree with them. The Abbasids were losing control of the people to the *ulama*. The Abbasids started to rely militarily on mercenary Turks for their army. The *ulama* continued to effectively undermine the monarchy; not to transfer power from the monarchy to the general community of Muslims, but to accrete power to themselves.

More *ulama* driven theologies developed. The Shiite developed different schools like the Sufi, some being mystical. The symbol of an infallible Imam remained important to the Shiites and after the eleventh Imam died in 874, his believed-to-exist infant son could not be found. That son became known as the "hidden" Twelfth Imam, and gave rise to the group of Shiites known as Twelvers.

The Shiite *ulama* effectively ruled their society as a sort of "agent" of the hidden Imam. When the normal range of human life expectancies passed for the hidden Imam, the "agent" *ulama* brought the message that Allah had concealed the hidden Imam and he would return to rule some time in the future. In the meantime, the Shiite *ulama* ruled in the hidden Imam's name.

There were also other groups of Shiites having somewhat different beliefs. So too with the Sunni. The internal strife also extended to the arts and sciences, which were distrusted by the more traditional *ulama*. After all, the reason and logic of Greek philosophy was like a new faith, to be opposed by the traditionalist. Yet, other schools honoring "reason" sprung up amongst Muslims. Mysticism also become popular and Sufism became important in Islam perhaps as a reaction to the stifling effects of the strict rules of the Shariah. The Sufis were said to have brought the "love" of Jesus into Islam.

Internal strife and wars ensued and soon the Abbasid Empire started to lose control of territory as strong factions arose in different parts of the empire. The Abbasid Empire fell apart, the strongest Muslim sect in an area taking control. The Turkish officers of the Abbasid armies started to take over, and in 1055 nailed-down their victory by capturing Baghdad. This finished the Abbasid Empire and power effectively passed to others, with the Turks being foremost.

## TURKS, AYYUBID DYNASTY & THE CRUSADES
   (1055-1258)

The Turks became Muslims, but as soldiers they were content to leave most matters in the hands of the *ulama*. By that time, the *ulama* had established educational institutions formalizing the continuation of their diverse views. The *ulama* ran the Shariah courts and had the effective ruling power.

Still more religious factions arose and both the political and religious situation became even more volatile for the Turks, until the ball game changed. The Crusaders attacked Jerusalem in 1099. It was almost 100 years before Jerusalem was retaken by Saladin, a Kurd who founded the Ayyubid dynasty.

That dynasty lasted about 50 years until the Mongols came on the scene. The Mongols completed their conquest of Islam by about 1258 when Baghdad was occupied and looted.

The path from the four caliphs to the Mongols was highlighted by the increasing presence and effectiveness of *ulama* sects. It started with the murder of Ali by the Kharijite, who themselves fell by the wayside as the *ulama* sects appeared and disappeared. The first dynasty, the Umayyads, gave way to the Abbasids and then to the

253

Ayyubids. The dynasties came to an end in the 13<sup>th</sup> century when Islam was conquered by a pagan nation, the Mongols.

One can draw many conclusions from this history and as I have shown, I ascribe the difficulties of Islam to those of its *ulama* who allowed the religion to be torn apart by sects that others of the *ulama* created, both in contradiction to the Koran; he one for creating the sects and the other for allowing it. The number and diversity of the sects were huge, going from the Assassins to the Zendiks. Perhaps it was no more extensive than the denominations in other religions, but the bloodletting may have been.

## MONGOLS, OTTOMAN & THE WEST (1258 on)

The Mongols ruled tolerantly, allowing all religions to worship as they pleased. The Mongols themselves eventually adopted Islam, but they stopped the *ulama* and their use of the Shariah, which the Mongols realized would impinge on the Mongol ability to rule. The Mongols had learned the lessons of history. They astutely realized that the imposition of the Shariah on a society effectively passed control of that society to the *ulama*.

The *ulama* response to being stymied by the Mongols was internalizing or tightening-up so as to preserve what they had achieved. They still controlled the religious sphere and became much more restrictive and religiously oppressive. In so doing, they finally stopped the innovation in the arts and sciences. And so, the light of the world was extinguished by the *ulama* after having been emblazoned some 400 years earlier by a secular ruler.

By the year 1400, Tamburlaine conquered some of the areas controlled by the now tame Mongols, but he was killed as he tried to expand into China. The Muslim Ottoman, the Turks of old who had adopted Islam, were also at work at during this period of time in conquering different areas of Islam, conquering part of Byzantium, advancing into the Balkans and Kosovo and finally, in 1453, capturing the prized Constantinople. In the meantime, Muslim merchants traveled the world and preached the faith, and eventually Islam was freely adopted in parts of Asia.

By the early 1500s, the Safavids ruled in Iran, the Mongols in Northern India, and the Ottoman in Turkey, Syria, Arabia, and parts of Western Europe and North Africa. The Safavids were Shiite and they began killing the Sunni in their midst and attacking them outside of Iran. In about 200 years, Iran was almost entirely Shiite.

The Shiite *ulama* continued representing the "hidden' Imam and began to claim an intermediary position between the ordinary Muslim community and Allah, and even used the Shariah to legislate new law that was binding on the secular ruler. The *ulama* effectively took control, laying the groundwork for future generations of *ulama*. After periods of secular control, the Ayatollah Khomeini took control of Iran in the 20th Century.

The Mongol empire in India was tolerant as the Mongols tended to be. All religions were given religious freedom and the Mongols actually helped them all. The poll tax on non-Muslims was eliminated. The Mongols, themselves Muslims by this time, tended toward the mysticism and love of the Sufi. The *ulama* were uncomfortable with these departures from the Shariah and the *ulama* soon wrested control, suppressing the Sufi and the other faiths and reinstating the poll tax. The Hindus were especially discriminated against, and eventually civil war ensued -- war again, courtesy of the *ulama*.

The Mongol empire in India fell apart in the middle of the 18th century and the Hindus and Muslims started to deal with each other. The Sikhs and the British became factors and the Muslims wound up, for the first time, under a tolerant state run by unbelievers. The Muslims lost their power, but they were no longer being manipulated by the *ulama*.

The Ottoman followed the Safavid model, but, being Sunni, they killed the Shiite amongst them and attacked the Safavids. Otherwise, the Ottoman practiced tolerance in the Mongol model, allowing all groups to live in peace and practice their own religions. Art and science started to flourish again under the Ottoman.

Although the Ottoman was stopped in their Western advances in Vienna, they remained the most powerful empire. The Shariah was implemented in the Ottoman Empire, but with the twist that the Ottoman rulers controlled the *ulama*. The *ulama* worked for the Ottoman and each legitimized each other in the usual style. The Ottoman collected the taxes and managed the society, but spread administrative power away from the *ulama* and out to many groups and, in so doing, diluted the traditional status, power and influence of the *ulama*.

In the 18th century, the Ottoman Empire started to fall apart. With the Wahhabi taking control in Arabia, the *ulama* were back in power there. In North Africa, the existing Sufi bias and a reaction against the backwardness attributed to the local *ulama* resulted in different kinds of Muslim states being carved out of the Ottoman Empire in Morocco and Libya.

The West overtook the Muslim world, particularly in the sciences that aided its colonial bent. The Ottoman Empire fell into decline on all fronts, as did the Safavid and Mongol empires. All the Muslim empires were in decline as the West advanced, just as the Muslims had advanced a thousand years earlier and the West fell into decline.

While it appears that Islam, at least in its expansionary

days, was violent in attacking others and also violent internally, it would be very difficult and very subjective to compare its violence with the violence of other religions in their pre-modern periods. Perhaps Islam was worse, perhaps not, but it is clear that they were not of like-kind.

Islam was successful in war, spectacularly successful. Perhaps there is a tendency for nomadic peoples with a fighting tradition to be "harder" than city folk and have a significant advantage in war, before the modern era. Note that after Islam settled-down and became city-soft, it was successfully invaded by other nomadic tribes, the Mongols, Turks, and also Tamburlaine. But this has little significance for present purposes.

What is significant is that, contrary to popular belief, there is no evidence that Muslims set out on a religious quest to conquer the world -- its expansionary wars were not religiously driven. Eventually, many of the conquered peoples adopted Islam, for economic or political reasons if not religious reasons, but little of the actual conversions can be ascribed to force.

While Islam is tainted with a warlike brush, it was the most tolerant in how it dealt with captured people. Religious intolerance arose in Christianity while Islam remained tolerant.

The violence of Islam was in violation of its Scripture,

not in pursuance of its Scripture. The Koran forbids war in many of the situations where Muslims had gone to war. This doesn't make Islam any the less violent, but the Koran itself does not call for this violence. The Koran itself is fundamentally anti-violence.

The Koran would make Islam a House of Peace, but it cannot really be called that because there is a vast disconnect between the dictates of the Koran and the practice. That disconnect can be lain at the door of some of Islam's learned religious leaders, the extremist *ulama*. Do not blame ordinary Muslims for the disconnect, although those in a position to counter the extremist *ulama* and those of *ulama* who are not extremists could be faulted under the Koran for not countering the extremists more.

# KORANIC VERSES

# Selected Koranic Verses

## and Index

The Koran was revealed in Arabic, and is said to be beautifully written, almost poetic. The author used English language translations which lose the poetry and but do not lose the meaning. A number of translations were consulted so as to arrive at what the author took as the gist (substance, essence, or general idea) of the verses listed. Thus, the text shown here does not represent direct quotations from the Koran, but embodies what the author believes to be the essential thoughts in those verses, written in English, in a modern style. While a few English translations of the Koran were compared so as to better understand these verses, accuracy can only be assured by reading the Koran in Arabic. Just a small portion of the more than 6,000 verses in the Koran are included here.

The bold, italicized letters and numbers that follow represent the author's text and the traditional numeric references to Koranic verses. The non-bold, non-italicized numbers represent the page numbers in this book where the Koranic verses are referred to.

**2.62**      *Whoever believes in God and the Last Day and does good, whether he be Muslim, Jew, Christian or Sabian, shall have their reward and should have no fear nor grieve on judgment day.* Pages 24, 43, 162, 165, 192, 209, 213.

**2.78**      *Those who lack knowledge and understanding know the Scripture only through hearsay and do nothing but guess.* Page 154.

**2.106**     *Whatever revelation Allah abrogates or causes to be disregarded in the old Scriptures, Allah brings one like it or better.* Pages 70, 167.

**2.125**     *Allah made His House a safe place for men to meet and pray in the place Abraham prayed after he and Ishmael cleared all the idols.* Page 223.

**2.126**     *Abraham asked Allah to make the region of Mecca a secure city of peace and feed its people.* Page 225.

**2.127**     *Abraham and Ishmael raised the foundations of the Kaba, the House of God, and asked Allah to accept it from them.* Page 225.

**2.128**     *Abraham and Ishmael asked Allah to make them Muslims and make from their offspring a nation submissive to Allah.* Page 225.

**2.129**     *Abraham and Ishmael petitioned Allah to raise up a messenger from among the people who shall recite the messages of Allah to the people and instruct them in Scripture and wisdom.* Page 63.

**2.136**     *Muslims believe in Allah and the revelations in the Koran and in the revelations to Abraham,*

*Ishmael, Isaac, Jacob and the tribes of Israel, Moses, Jesus, and to all the other prophets, and do not distinguish between any of them.* Pages 18, 23, 41, 67, 216.

*2.141* *The ancient Jews and Christians have passed away and theirs is what they had earned, while their progeny earn what is theirs and are not to be asked what their ancestors did.* Pages 14, 25, 44, 206, 215, 216, 218.

*2.143* *Allah has made Muslims an exalted nation in the middle of the world and a teacher of nations.* Page 217.

*2.144* *Wherever you are, turn your faces to the Sacred Mosque when you pray.* Page 222.

*2.145* *Muslims cannot follow the direction of prayer of the People of the Book.* Page 222.

*2.151* *Allah sent you a messenger from amongst you to recite His revelations and teach you Scripture and wisdom.* Page 76.

*2.172* *You should eat of the good things that Allah has provided for you.* Page 35.

*2.177* *Out of their love for Allah, the righteous give of their wealth to near kin, to orphans, to the needy, to wayfarers, to those who ask, and to set slaves free.* Page 35.

*2.178-179* *Under the law of equality, the retaliation prescribed for murder is death for death; but if instead requested by the victim's brother, compensation is payable.* Page 137.

*2.228*　　*Women have rights against their husbands similar to the rights their husbands have against them, but men are a degree above women.* Pages 30, 32.

*2.256*　　*There should be no compulsion in religion.* Pages 22, 34, 54, 137, 175.

*3.3*　　*Allah has revealed to the Koran to you, and verifies that He also revealed the Torah and Gospel.* Pages 18, 22, 40, 67, 93, 167, 192, 215, 217.

*3.7*　　*The Koran consists of two types of verses. There are the basic verses of substance that have clear and established meaning. The others are allegorical verses the meanings of which are known only to Allah and cannot be known by man, and yet man causes discord by seeking to explain them.* Pages 100, 169.

*3.20*　　*If the people of the Book and the unlearned people turn their backs on submitting to Islam, your duty is only to have delivered the message.* Pages 22, 45, 137.

*3.25*　　*On the day of judgment, every person will be paid in full what that person had earned.* Page 168.

*3.103*　　*Keep your bond to Allah and be all together, not disunited.* Pages 83, 96, 170, 186, 210.

*3.105*　　*Do not disagree and become divided in religion.* Page 83.

*3.108*　　*Allah wills no injustice to any creature of His.* Page 23.

*3.113-5*　　*People of a group are not all alike. There*

*are those amongst the People of Book who are upright, believe in God and the Last Day and recite His messages throughout the night; they are righteous and their good deeds will not be denied them.* Pages 44, 191, 214.

*3.138* *The Koran is a clear statement.* Pages 10, 78, 156.

*3.185* *Every person will receive their reward only on the day of judgment.* Pages 15, 163.

*3.195* *Those who were driven from their homes, fought in Allah's way and were slain will enter Paradise.* Page 165.

*3.198* *Those who do their duty to Allah will go to Paradise.* Page 165.

*4.3* *Marry even two, three or four woman if you feel that you can treat them justly.* Page 32.

*4.7* *Both men and women can inherit the property of parents and near relatives.* Page 30.

*4.19* *Women are not inheritable nor may their dowry be taken back against their will.* Page 29.

*4.29* *Do not kill yourselves.* Pages 19, 163, 186.

*4.32* *Allah has given more to some of you, which you should not covet. Both men and women shall have the benefit of what they earn.* Pages 30, 32, 35, 35.

*4.34* *Men have the obligations to protect and maintain women because Allah has given them greater strength and wealth to support them.* Pages 8, 30, 32.

180, 192, 214

**4.135** *Stand fast for justice and as bearers of witness even against yourself, parents, relatives or friends, rich or poor.* Pages 23, 88.

**4.124** *Believers, whether male or female, who do good deeds will be admitted to Paradise and treated equitably.* Page 30.

**4.146** *Non-believers who repent, changing their ways and holding fast to Allah, will be accepted as believers.* Page 193.

**5.3** *This day Allah perfected your religion for you and completed His favor to you by choosing Islam as your religion.* Pages 66, 217.

**5.5** *It is lawful for Muslims to eat the food of Jews and Christians and marry their chaste women.* Pages 41, 193.

**5.8** *Be steadfast in fair dealing, and do not let hatred of a people induce you into doing wrong and depart from justice.* Page 220.

**5.13** *Do not alter words from their context nor neglect a portion of what the Koran says.* Pages 100, 112, 157, 211.

**5.32** *Whoever killed a human being (unless as punishment for murder or treason), it shall be as though he slew all mankind; and whoever saved a life, it shall be as though he saved all mankind.* Pages 11, 157.

**5.48** *Allah revealed to you the Koran and verifies the previous Scriptures He revealed before it, and*

*Allah stands guard over all of them. Allah could have chosen to make all the peoples a single people, but made them as they are in order to try them as they vie with one another in good works.* Pages 18, 21, 22, 41, 67, 96, 167.

5.63    *Why don't the rabbis and the priests forbid the mocker's evil-speaking and their devouring illicit gain?* Page 218.

5.87    *You should not forbid the good things which Allah has made lawful for believers.* Pages 31, 35, 111.

5.97    *Allah has made the Kaba, the Sacred House, a secure asylum for the people.* Page 223.

6.2    *Allah created you from clay and then decreed a fixed lifespan for you.* Pages 19, 162.

6.15    *Muslims who disobey Allah should fear the retribution of a grievous day.* Pages 111, 139.

6.32    *Life on earth is play and sport, with the Hereafter being a better abode for believers.* Page 166.

6.50    *I [Muhammad] don't have the treasures of Allah, don't know the unseen, and I'm not an angel. I follow only what is revealed to me.* Pages 26, 76.

6.52    *Although you are not accountable to other believers for anything and they are not accountable to you for anything, do not drive other believers away from Allah.* Page 97.

6.114    *The Koran was sent to you explained in full detail.* Pages 10, 64, 72, 78, 100.

26, 76, 141.

**8.15**        *Do not flee before unbelievers marching against you in war.* Pages 136, 166, 195.

**8.19**        *Desist from fighting the enemy if the enemy desists; return to fighting if the enemy returns to the attack.* Pages 54, 142, 161.

**8.46**        *Obey Allah and do not enter into disputes with one another.* Page 139.

**8.60**        *Use whatever force you can muster and all your strength against your enemy in war to strike fear into them.* Page 136.

**8.61**        *If the enemy is inclined to peace, you should also be inclined to peace.* Pages 54, 142.

**8.69**        *Enjoy what you have lawfully won in war.* Page 35.

**9.5**        *Fight and kill pagans wheresoever you find them, seize them as captives, beleaguer them, and lie in wait to ambush them.* Pages 112, 159, 208, 209.

**9.11**        *Those who turn into believers, pray regularly and give charity become your brothers in faith.* Page 97.

**9.13**        *Fight those pagans who violated their oaths, assailed your religion and attacked you first.* Pages 112, 159, 208.

**9.28**        *Pagans, being unclean, are forbidden to come near the Sacred Mosque.* Page 204.

**9.31**        *Do not take the doctors of law and the very pious as you would your Lord.* Pages 126, 141.

**9.34**        *Beware of the doctors of law and the very*

*pious who falsely waste your charity and deprive you of funds for true charity in Allah's way.* Pages 126, 141.

*9.36* **Fight all together as they fight you all together; but know that Allah is with those who restrain themselves.** Pages 170, 186, 210, 211.

*9.38* **Do not cling to life on earth which is little compared to the Hereafter.** Page 166.

*9.44* **Believer should not ask for an exemption from fighting with their wealth and persons.** Page 166.

*9.111* **In a promise binding on Allah in the Torah, Gospel and Koran, Allah admits to Paradise believers who devote their persons and their property fighting in God's way.** Pages 24, 42, 192.

*9.119* **Believers should keep their duty to Allah by being truthful.** Page 203.

*10.1* **These, the verses of the Koran, are the verses of the Book of Wisdom.** Pages 64, 76.

*10.25* **Allah invites whom He will to the abode of peace, and guides those He pleases to the right path.** Page 37.

*10.37* **The Koran is a confirmation and fuller explanation of the Scriptures previously revealed by Allah.** Page 167.

*11.1* **The Koran is a Book of wisdom made plain.** Page 100.

*11.118* **If Allah had so wanted, He could have made all mankind a single people.** Page 21.

107, 157.

**17.32** *Do not go near fornication as it is an obscenity.* Page 168.

**17.93** *I [Muhammad] am only a mortal man, a messenger.* Pages 26, 76, 140.

**18.29** *Allah has provided the truth and man is free to believe or disbelieve.* Pages 21, 34.

**18.49** *Allah will be unjust to no one.* Page 23.

**21.47** *Allah will justly balance a person's good and evil deeds so as to not wrong anyone in the slightest degree on the day of judgment.* Pages 14, 107, 157.

**22.25** *Allah has made the Sacred Mosque open to all of mankind [who adopt Islam].* Page 204.

**22.39** *Allah permits Muslins to fight if war is first made on them.* Pages 11, 135, 159, 186, 194.

**22.40** *But for Allah's protection, monasteries, churches, synagogues and mosques where God's name is often mentioned would have been torn down.* Pages 41, 193.

**22.78** *Strive hard (jihad) in Allah's cause as you ought to strive, establishing regular prayer, giving regular charity, and holding fast to Him. Allah has chosen you for His religion and has named you Muslims.* Pages 66, 158, 217.

**24.2** *The man and woman guilty of adultery shall be flogged, each with a hundred stokes.* Page 33.

**24.30-31** *Believing men and women should lower their gazes and act modestly.* Page 32.

**24.31** *Women should not display their naked*

adornments except to husbands, fathers, sons and sisters and children who know nothing about women's nakedness. Head-coverings could be used to cover their bosoms. Page 31.

25.32      The Koran was not revealed all at once, and Allah arranged for it to be in the right order. Pages 63, 66.

25.68      Those who should fear penalty on the day of judgment are those who commit adultery, or slay a life made sacred by Allah except in the way of Allah's law and justice, or worship another god. Page 158.

26.192-5      The Koran is a revelation from Allah, brought by the Faithful Spirit [the angel Gabriel] in plain Arabic. Page 63.

27.91      Allah made the city of Mecca sacred. Page 203.

29.46      Muslims should not argue with people of the Book in other than helpful ways, except for those of them who do wrong, and tell them that we Muslims believe in the revelations to us and in the revelations to you, and that our God and your God is the same one God. Pages 24, 41, 67, 217.

29.67      Allah secured the sacred territory of Mecca from violence. Page 203.

31.2-4      This is the Book of Wisdom, its verses a guide and mercy for the doers of good who establish regular prayer, offer regular charity and are certain of the Hereafter. Pages 64, 76.

32.17      No person knows what delights await in

*Paradise.*  Page 169.

*33.21*        *The messenger of Allah [Muhammad] is an excellent exemplar for those who follow and praise Allah.*  Pages 64, 76.

*33.40*        *Muhammad is the messenger of Allah and the last of the prophets.*  Pages 63, 66, 88, 120.

*33.70*        *Believers should keep their duty to Allah by speaking straight words.*  Page 160.

*36.51*        *When the trumpet is sounded, the dead will rise from their graves and hasten unto Allah.*  Pages 15, 163.

*38.20*        *Allah strengthened his [King David's] kingdom and gave him sound judgment and wisdom to help him rule.*  Pages 69, 71, 92, 108.

*38.26*        *Allah made you [King David] a ruler on earth, so judge justly and do not follow personal desires.*  Page 92.

*40.39*        *Life in this world is only an enjoyment, and the Hereafter is the abode to settle in.*  Page 166.

*42.15*        *God is our Lord and your Lord.  For us are our deeds and for you your deeds, and there is no argument between us, and God will eventually gather us together.*  Pages 21, 43.

*42.38*        *Affairs should be decided by taking counsel amongst yourselves.*  Pages 28, 71, 86, 88, 93, 95, 108, 142.

*45.14*        *Believers should forgive those who do not believe.*  Pages 45, 191.

*46.2*        *The revelations of the Koran are from Allah.*

Page 139.

**46.9** *I [Muhammad] wasn't the first messenger and I don't know what will be done with me or you. I follow only what is revealed to me, and I'm only a deliverer of warnings.* Pages 26, 76.

**46.15** *When man reaches forty years of age, he starts to give thanks to Allah.* Page 62.

**47.15** *This is a parable of Paradise promised to the dutiful: therein are rivers of water incorruptible, rivers of milk of unchanging taste; rivers of wine delicious to drinkers, and rivers of honey pure and clear.* Pages 17, 36, 169.

**49.6** *If a person comes to you with a report, look carefully into the truth lest you harm someone unawares and afterwards be sorry for your actions.* Pages 13, 157.

**49.9** *If parties of believers quarrel, make peace between them with fairness and justice. If one party does wrong to the other, fight the one who does wrong until they obey Allah.* Pages 20, 52, 138, 154, 181, 210.

**49.10** *All believers are brethren and you have a duty to make peace between your contending brethren.* Pages 20, 52, 96, 138, 154, 179, 210.

**49.13** *Mankind was created from a single pair, male and a female, and made into tribes and nations so that they might know one another.* Page 96.

**49.14** *Those who submit to Islam should be accepted as Muslims even if faith hasn't yet entered*

*forth what is in it, those who strove hard for Allah will be joyful and the others will go into the burning fires of perdition.* Page 163.

**89.21-23** *On the day when the earth crumbles to pieces and Allah comes with angels, hell will be made to appear and man will remember his record.* Page 164.

**109.1-6** *I have my religion and you have yours and we each have our own recompense.* Pages 21, 34.

# KORANIC VERSES

# References

TRANSLATIONS OF THE KORAN

*The Holy Qur'an, Arabic Text with English Translation and Commentary*, by Maulana Muhammad Ali (d.1951), Ahmadiyya Anjuman Isha'at Islam Lahore Inc., Dublin, Ohio, USA, first edition 1917, 2002 edition.

*The Holy Qur'an, Text, Translation and Commentary*, by Abdullah Yusuf Ali, Tahrike Tarsile Qur'an, Elmhurst, New York, 2005.

*The Glorious Qur'an, Text and Explanatory Translation*, by Muhammad M. Pickthall, Tahrike Tarsile Qur'an, Elmhurst, New York, Second U.S. Edition, 1999.

# TRANSLATION OF THE HEBREW BIBLE / OLD TESTAMENT

*The Holy Bible, King James Version, 1611.*

# OTHER REFERENCES

Ahmed, Akbar S., *DISCOVERING ISLAM, Making Sense of Muslim History and Society*, Routledge, London, 1988, revised edition 2002.

Armstrong, Karen, *ISLAM, A Short History*, Random House, New York, 2000.

Berkey, Jonathan P., *THE FORMATION of ISLAM, Religion and Society in the Near East, 600-1800*, Cambridge University Press, 2003.

Berman, Paul, *Terror and Liberalism*, W. W. Norton, New York, 2003.

Brockopp, Jonathan E., Editor, *Islamic Ethics of Life, Abortion, War, and Euthanasia*, University of South Carolina Press, Columbia, South Carolina, 2003.

Crone, Patricia, *Roman, Provincial and Islamic Law: The Origins Of the Islamic Patronate*, Cambridge

University Press, 1987.

Esposito, John L., *Unholy War, Terror in the name of Islam*, Oxford University Press, 2002. *What Everyone Needs to Know About Islam*, Oxford University Press, 2002.

Ezzati, A., *THE SPREAD OF ISLAM, The Contributing Factors*, Islamic College for Advanced Studies Press, London, 2002.

Feldman, Noah, *After Jihad, America and the Struggle for Islamic Democracy*, Farrar, Straus and Giroux, New York City, 2003.

Fluehr-Lobban, Carolyn, Editor, *Against Islamic Extremism, The Writings of Muhammad Sa'id al-Ashmawy*, University Press of Florida, 1998.

Gray, John, *AL QAEDA and what it means to be modern*, Faber and Faber, London, The New Press, New York City, 2003.

Hafez, Mohammed M., *WHY MUSLIMS REBEL, Repression and Resistance in the Ilamic World*, Lynne Rienner Publishers, Boulder, Colorado, 2003.

Ibn Warraq, Editor and Translator, *The Quest for the Historical Muhammad*, Prometheus Books, New York,

2000.

Kepel, Giles, *Al Qaeda in Its Own Words*, Harvard University Press, Cambridge, 2008.

Khadduri, Majid, *The Islamic Conception of Justice*, Johns Hopkins University Press, Baltimore, 1984.

Khare, R. S., Editor, *Perspectives on Islamic Law, Justice, and Society*, Rowman & Littlefield, Lanham, Maryland, 1999.

Lewis, Bernard, *The Crises of Islam, Holy War and Unholy Terror,* Random House Modern Library, New York, 2003. *What Went Wrong? Western Impact and Middle Eastern Response*, Oxford University Press, 2002. *The Shaping of the Modern Middle East*, Oxford University Press, 1964, 1994. *The Jews of Islam*, Princeton University Press, 1984

Moussalli, Ahmad S., Editor, *Islamic Fundamentalism, Myths & Realities*, Garnet Publishing, Reading, UK, 1998.

Power, Samantha, *"A Problem From Hell," America and the Age of Genocide*, Basic Books, New York City, 2002.

Rosen, Lawrence, *The Justice of Islam, Comparative*

*Perspectives on Islamic Law and Society*, Oxford University Press, 2000.

Saad-Ghorayeb, Amal, *HIZBU'LLAH, Politics and Religion*, Pluto Press, London, 2002.

Schimmel, Annemarie, *ISLAM, An Introduction*, State University of New York Press, 1992.

Schwartz, Steven, *The Two Faces of Islam, The House of Sa'ud from Tradition to Terror*, Doubleday, New York, 2002.

Scruton, Roger, *The West and the Rest, Globalization and the Terrorist Threat*, ISI Books, Wilmington, Delaware, 2002.

Stern, Jessica, *Terror in the Name of God, Why Religious Militants Kill*, Harper Collins, New York City, 2003.

Torrey, Charles Cutler, *The Jewish Foundation of Islam*, KTAV Publishing House, New York, 1967, first published 1933.

Zakaria, Fareed, *THE FUTURE OF FREEDOM, Illiberal Democracy at Home and Abroad*, W. W. Norton & Company, New York, 2003.

# KORANIC VERSES

# Index

2403225

Made in the USA